The Mexican Ame

The Mexican American

PERSPECTIVES
ON MEXICAN-AMERICAN LIFE

ARNO PRESS
A New York Times Company
New York — 1974

0730062

Reprint Edition 1974 by Arno Press Inc.

The Near Side of the Mexican Question is
Copyright, 1921, by George H. Doran Company
The Near Side of the Mexican Question is
reprinted by permission of Doubleday and Company

The Near Side of the Mexican Question was reprinted
from a copy in The Newark Public Library
How Mexicans Earn and Live was reprinted from
a copy in The University of Illinois Library

THE MEXICAN AMERICAN
ISBN for complete set: 0-405-05670-2
See last pages of this volume for titles.

Manufactured in the United States of America

Library of Congress Cataloging in Publication Data
Main entry under title:.

Perspectives on Mexican-American life.

(The Mexican American)
Reprint of the 1920 ed. of The Mexican housing
problem, by E. Fuller, published by Southern California
Sociological Society, Los Angeles, of the 1921 ed. of
The near side of the Mexican question, by J. S. Stowell,
published by G. H. Doran Co., New York, and of the 1933
ed. of How Mexicans earn and live, by the University of
California Heller Committee for Research in Social
Economics, published by the University of California
Press, Berkeley.
    1. Mexican Americans. 2. Mexican Americans--
California. 3. Mexicans in the United States.
I. Fuller, Elizabeth. The Mexican housing problem in
Los Angeles. 1974. II. Stowell, Jay Samuel. The
near side of the Mexican question. 1974. III. Cali-
fornia. University. Heller Committee for Research
in Social Economics. Cost of living studies: v. How
Mexicans earn and live. 1974. IV. Series.
E184.M5P43 1974   917.3'06'6872   73-14214
ISBN 0-405-05688-5

CONTENTS

INTRODUCTION

This anthology provides three perspectives on Mexican-American life in the 1920's and 1930's. Two of the selections focus on localized California subjects—housing problems faced by Mexicans in Los Angeles and the incomes and expenditures of Mexicans in San Diego. The other—Jay S. Stowell's *The Near Side of the Mexican Question*—takes a broader view of Mexican people in the U.S.

Despite the variety of subject matter and perspectives, the three books have at least one common feature—all three suffer, to some degree, from ethnocentrism and cultural insensitivity—traits which unfortunately still characterize much of the scholarship on the Mexican American. Yet, despite these limitations, the three studies in this anthology are still valuable. Not only are they useful sources of information, but they also serve as interesting examples of older scholarly and journalistic treatments and mistreatments of the Mexican American.

Dr. Carlos E. Cortes
University of California,
Riverside

THE MEXICAN HOUSING PROBLEM
IN LOS ANGELES

By ELIZABETH FULLER, A. B.

THE MEXICAN HOUSING PROBLEM IN LOS ANGELES

By ELIZABETH FULLER, A. B.

Due to the rapid industrial growth of Los Angeles, thousands of Mexicans are being attracted to it yearly and the housing of these people becomes a current problem. Los Angeles, however, is doing little towards the solving of it. Even the people who have lived in Los Angeles long enough to realize the seriousness of the Mexican housing problem carelessly dismiss it with the Mexican's own characteristic expression, "Manana." In fact, we seldom think of the Mexican at all, and when we do, it is to picture him a heavy-lipped, sleepy-eyed Latin reclining in the sun, too lazy to seek the shade. Memory recalls a picturesque sombrero partially concealing the straight black hair of his race, a bandana of scarlet knotted about his neck, and a sleeping dog, scant of hair curled at his feet. Few persons stop to consider that behind those dull eyes lies the tragedy of a nation, that his idleness is due to lack of mental development—the result of the years of oppression—and that his contentment with so little is but the heritage of generations who have been forced to adapt themselves to bitter poverty and insupportable tyranny. On the other hand we have caught the contagious shrug and with a lift of our shoulders exclaim, "The Mexican is a problem of tomorrow!"

The feeling of the level-minded social worker, who abhors hasty decisions and unfounded statements, is that the Mexican situation in Los Angeles at present, is not inconceivably horrible,

Editor's Note—Miss Elizabeth Fuller received the degree of Bachelor of Arts from the University of Southern California, June, 1920, with a "Major" in Sociology. She was a resident at the Neighborhood Settlement House, 1919-1920, during which time she secured the data, on the basis of which this monograph was prepared. She is under appointment for Social Service work in China.

1

but that the conditions, if taken in time can be greatly improved. I chose for this study fifty Mexican homes between Wilson street and the Los Angeles River on East Ninth, and on Channing street between Ninth and Fourteenth streets. Systematically, I have visited from house to house. The frank courtesy and ready wit, the unrestrained gratitude and affection of the Mexican have made my task an easy one. After reviewing the data gathered, I do not feel discouraged. True, I have been made aware of the lax moral standards of the race, and the child-like disregard of our standard of marriage and parental responsibility. Only too often have I found the mother and the state of California taking the responsibility of an absent father. Unmarried Mexican mothers are not uncommon. Yet the Mexican mother represents the strength of her race. Patient, industrious, honest, sympathetic and loving, she sacrifices herself without stint for her children. Since the home, strictly speaking, includes the father, mother and children, it has been difficult to tabulate the "number of families per house," when the father is not present as a member of the family. Two unmarried mothers with their children are frequently housed together. With the exception of this confusion I believe that the data which I present is correct.

Instinctively, the Mexicans huddle together in certain districts. Since any one district can contain only a certain number of houses in a block, it is not unusual to find two or three families housed under one roof; within a house that contains not over four or five rooms. Moreover, Mexican hospitality invites cousins, uncles, and aunts to room and board with the fortunate possessor of a shelter. Three beds to a room, even four, the children sleeping on the floor, a very poor make-shift of a stove, no electric lights, no plumbing, no furniture, and the ever present trunk constitute the courteous Mexican's hospitality to his immigrant relatives. Then, perhaps, the heads of the various families gain employment. The first pay envelope means a "fiesta" for the entire household. The rooms, bare of furniture, are garnished with ferns. Music, loud talking, and pleasant compliments are heard and exchanged. Frijoles and tortillas are in abundance. A string of shiny beads is bought for the "nina." A fifteen cent ring for the "muchacho," and a bracelet for the cousin's child. Accustomed to very little in Mexico, the Mexican accepts the very worst in the way of a home that Los Angeles has to offer him. Often he sees no reason why he should improve the home

2

which has been granted him. An old store building, an abandoned, neglected mill, a tumbled-down house—with these the Mexican is usually content.

Conditions among Fifty Mexican Families.

TABLE I.

Average number of families per house	1.30
Average number of persons per house	5.78
Average number of adults per house	2.68
Average number of children per house	3.10
Average weekly wage per family	$24.11
Average monthly rent per house	$9.80
Average number of rooms per house	3.32
Average rent paid per room	$2.85
Average size of rooms	10 ft. x 8 ft.
Average number of beds per family	2.25
Average number of individuals per bed	2.52

The word "court" to the school-teacher and city nurse spells all that is horrible and filthy. The court or "patio" in itself is not an evil, but indeed, a survival of the Mexican social instinct. Several houses grouped about an open space is a beautiful heritage from Spain. Friendliness and neighborliness are promoted. But when unscrupulous landlords provide but one toilet for the entire court, allow any number of people to live in one small two-room house, and charge exorbitant rent for this lack of convenience and decency, the court is an evil and a menace to Los Angeles.

One house particularly repulsive is that of the Garnica (fictitious name) family. A father, a mother, a grandmother, a sister-in-law, four children, and a baby are sheltered by the walls of an abandoned water mill, one room on the ground floor, and a room up in the loft. A prehistoric stove adds heat to the overmoist air and carbon dioxide. Both windows are nailed down, but the door is fortunately loose from the hinges. A water faucet, very new, coquettishly glistens four or five feet above the floor on the far side of the room. A bed, a chair, and a couple of soap-boxes are the furniture. The Italian neighbor allows the family to use his toilet—incidentally, he is sub-renting the mill, which happened to be on his lot, to this family at the rate of eleven dollars per month. The father earns twenty-five dollars a week and is willing to pay more rent for a better house, but cannot find one. Since the room containing the one bed in the house is parlor, play-room, kitchen and nursery, the city nurse insisted that the mother be removed elsewhere during

3

confinement. The father would not permit her to go to the hospital. As he had been in the country for only six months, he did not understand the convenience of a hospital. A kind-hearted Mexican woman, a stranger, with a baby only two months old, providentially offered a bed in her four room mansion.

In a court-like formation on East Ninth street, five houses share all sanitary conveniences with a bakery. Two houses—old store buildings—have two rooms each; one house, four rooms; and two, three. Trunks and beds again are the only furnishings. A rope swung across the doorway divides one family from another in the house of two rooms. Three beds are in each room. All experts on housing conditions agree that a house is overcrowded when there are more than two persons to each room and when there does not exist a space ten feet square and eight feet high for each individual. When six to nine people are living within two rooms, overcrowding exists.

The tabulated list of homes visited includes the homes of the recent immigrants, and reveals the worst conditions. The Mexican is not hopeless. He comes here as a young husband and a young father. He is anxious to make his children American. Trace the history of any Mexican family coming under the influence of church, school, mission, or settlement, and you will find steady improvement. When the Mexican first arrives, he is, according to our standards, dirty, shiftless, and lazy. His children go to school, to improvement clubs, to the mission, and it is to these institutions that the improvement in the home is due.

I have in mind a house rented by the Garcias (fictitious name). The windows were nailed down. Newspapers covered the spots on the wall, devoid of wall paper. The various trunks and one bed were placed together in one room of the seven-room house. Mr. and Mrs. Garcia and fourteen children were the number added to the population of Los Angeles by the advent of this family. Mrs. Garcia invented a table; boards were spread across the trunks. This table was not large enough for the entire family, so the younger children were allowed to eat first, and then were sent outside to play. The father and mother with the older brothers and sisters then had their family meal, an institution entirely unheard of by newly arrived Mexican immigrants. A can of unheated corn, frijoles, tortillas, and fruit served at odd intervals and whenever the family larder will provide constituted the ordinary meal. When the Garcia girls grew

4

older they worked in factories. Their earnings bought furniture, cheap and ornate, which with full length portraits, gives a home atmosphere to the parlor. Rope portieres now divide the parlor from the bedroom. From a corner a cheap phonograph furnishes music. Old lace curtains decorate the windows. Rugs, of a poor variety to be sure, cover the floor. The landlord has been forced to put in electric lights. The garden in the rear of the house adds to the prosperous appearance of the dwelling. The home breathes an atmosphere of peace and contentment. No longer is the inquisitive glance of the social visitor dreaded.

To the usual visitor, another family I have in mind has not progressed far, for at present, three-legged makeshift chairs and boxes comprise the furniture of the living room. But a closer acquaintance reveals very promising tendencies. Having neither electric lights nor gas, the mother has taught the children to keep the lamps clean and in order. Under no conditions are members of the family allowed to sleep in the room where the busy mother prepares and cooks the food. The father wishes to be known in the community as a man deserving of respect. His garden is profitable and well worth while, breathing a message of encouragement to the block of tumbled-down houses.

Conditions among Fifty Mexican Families.

TABLE II.

Houses sheltering more than one family	28%
Houses of less than three rooms	36%
Houses sheltering more than two persons per room	46%
Families paying more than $10.00 rent per month	42%
Families earning more than $24.00 per week	22%
Families earning less than $24.00 per week	64%
Families with more than two beds	30%
Families with less than two beds	40%
Families with more than two persons per bed	64%

The general impressions received by those who work among the Mexicans are varied in nature. The visitor finds a gate swung on springs (of a home manufacture), heavily weighted with a brick. Although the fence may possess wide spaces caused by lack of boards or laths, the visitor always finds the gate and the brick. After entering the yard she notices that the ground usually has been swept clean. Sticks have been picked up and burned. The bare adobe, baked in the California sun, is almost polished. Perhaps on the ground, in front of the delapidated steps, there will be cottolene

cans filled with dirt and sprigs of geranium.   As the visitor nears
the door a peculiar odor greets her. This, she finds out afterwards,
is due to lack of ventillation and to inadequate sanitary arrangements.   When she knocks at the door, a voice calls "Pase Vd,"
and the visitor enters.   Coming from bright daylight into a dark-
ened room, almost blinds the caller, the peculiar odor and the close-
ness prompt her to comment. "How awful! What terrible conditions!"   But as soon as her eyes become accustomed to the darkness
and her nostrils to the air, she discovers a very picturesque group.
Upon one of the beds, asleep, lies a naked infant. A couple of women
sit on the floor, and a man is seated on the most precious of all possessions to the Mexican immigrant—his "baul" or trunk. A virgin
and perhaps a saint, are placed on a shelf on the wall, before which
a short candle burns. Oddly decorated paper covers the wall, assisted
in patches by copies of the "Examiner" or "Times." A bed, two
beds, perhaps three, are in the various corners of the room. These
are covered with very poor—but clean—thinly padded quilts.
There are no sheets or pillow cases, and the ticking is as clean as
possible under the conditions. The floor is clean; indeed, the room
is remarkable for its absence of clutter. The accumulated trash,
characteristic of so many houses of the poor, is not found here. The
odor and close air and the darkness are due to the lack of education
in hygiene. The crowded conditions of the house, the poor construction, the lack of common conveniences are due to the greed
of the landlords, and a faulty economic system.

Conditions among Fifty Mexican Families.

TABLE III.

Houses with gas	8%
Houses without gas	92%
Houses with electricity	28%
Houses without electricity	72%
Houses with garden	8%
Houses with inside toilet	52%
Houses with outside toilet	18%
Houses with no toilet	30%
Families sharing toilet	24%

Condition of toilet—54% Good—12% Fair—34% Poor.

Los Angeles so far has considered the Mexican immigrant chiefly
as an industrial asset. He has been allowed to drift into the worst
sections of the city and to be exploited by the landlords. And what
has been the result? The city has been forced to increase her public
health staff. The damp, unsanitary, dark homes of the Mexicans

are a constant source of tuberculosis. Moreover, because of the crowded conditions, the social diseases are rapidly spreading among these people. Churches and missions, settlements and schools, feel that the lax standard of morals among the Mexicans can be dealt with in no other way than by providing better homes.

In Mexico, these people have lived huddled together in habitations of one or two rooms in the midst of indescribable filth. Women are chattels. Children are born diseased and feeble-minded. Lazy and shiftless, the Mexican has lived satisfied from day to day. Moreover, in our own city we are allowing the same conditions to develop. Crowded quarters, strangers living together in one house of two rooms, lack of sanitary arrangements—these produce moral degeneracy. Darkness and foul air are not the dwelling place of energy and ambition. If America is going to awake the latent powers of the Mexican, she cannot offer him miserable shacks for a shelter. Furthermore, she cannot afford to develop a race of beggars and paupers. The Mexican accepts what he is given. If he is housed in ill-drained buildings, buildings with insufficient light and air, with poor sanitary plumbing, and small rooms, he soon becomes the recipient of all manner of philanthropy. Philanthropy is not what the Mexican needs. He should be made self-reliant, proud of his own efficiency, and independent. But the environment such as Los Angeles is offering to the Mexican is not conducive to any moral reformation.

The young people among the Mexicans are a problem within themselves. Their homes are uninviting. No warmth and light means early retiring in the evening, which is characteristic of the Mexican, or else wandering about on the streets. No privacy is permitted the young Mexican man in the commonly overcrowded home. He is forced to go elsewhere for recreational activity. The monotony and dinginess of his shelter decrease the health, cheerfulness, and optimism of the adolescent boy. I have been appalled by the conversation of a seventeen year old Mexican boy. In the second year of high school, he confesses a desire for further education. I suggested a scholarship and college. "What's the use," he said, "when I come home I am all the more unhappy. The house is dark and cold. The children are under my feet, squalling and yelling. Mother never has time to talk with me, and my father goes to bed as soon as it is dark. We haven't even a decent room; the plaster is falling, and the roof leaks. I want to get out and work; and move out of that

7

hole. I might just as well be a bum and chase the streets, as be in the home I have." I was unable to answer him. His father earns four dollars and a half a day. There are ten in the family and Manuel is the oldest. I cannot help but think, however, that one important reason they have remained poor is the various "shacks" in which they have lived. If when they came to the city ten years ago, the city had offered them a well-built home, charging them what they could afford, Manuel would today be more ambitious.

This type of home is the means of manufacturing the boy criminal. There is no home pride; no family pride can develop. Without this family pride the child is not taught individual responsibility. He tries to get everything that he can for nothing. He shoots craps, gambles, steals, and refuses to attend school.

Conditions among Fifty Mexican Families.

TABLE IV.

	Good	Fair	Poor
Roof	10%	30%	60%
Paint	2%	10%	88%
Sun and Light	20%	26%	54%
Ventilation	32%	18%	50%
Drainage	8%	30%	62%
Cleanliness of Interior	26%	56%	18%
Cleanliness of Yard	70%	28%	2%

Do the Mexicans desire better homes? Yes and no. They are child-like in their desires. I asked one woman, who seemed to be more capable of comprehending than the average Mexican woman if she was satisfied with her home. She promptly said, "Yes." She neither complained of the rent nor of the character of the house. A couple of hours later, when returning, I passed this same place. The woman rushed out and in very excited Spanish wanted to know if I were an "inspectadora." She asked me to obtain for her pretty wall paper, paper with large and showy designs. That she had no bath-tub or range had not troubled her, but when thinking over what she really lacked, she decided that it was wall-paper, demonstrating the general aesthetic instinct which is characteristic of the Mexican. If the social worker were compelled to live in a dull, dingy bed-room or kitchen twenty-four hours a day, would not the very walls bore themselves deep into her consciousness? Her idea of interior decoration and that of the Mexican would differ, yet the instinct is the same.

The great evils in the present housing conditions are that the

8

average Mexican immigrant knows nothing better than his present conditions and that no desire for better living has been created. However, through the children the schools are teaching hygienic standards. The city nurses go into the home and give the mother instruction in sanitation. Missions and settlements conduct housekeeping classes for the young mother. Yet all these cannot offset the actual condition of the house in which the Mexican lives. It is in part the landlord's responsibility to provide better homes for the Mexican. It is his duty to make the homes as attractive as possible, to see that the plumbing is adequate, that there are several windows. It is his duty to see that the roof does not leak, that the house is well drained. It is a prerogative which he should not hand over to the Housing Commission. After providing the Mexican with a suitable dwelling, he should attempt to keep the tenant up to a certain standard. He should have in his employ certain agents whose duty it would be to visit and inspect the rented houses. The Mexican is very adaptable. If he understood that his money was not the only remuneration expected of him for his shelter, that he was expected to keep the house in good condition, and even improve it, he would soon adjust himself to the demands. The landlord at first objects and declares that this method incurs extra expense, yet eventually his would be the profit. The value of his investment would at least remain at par value or might even increase. Merely as a good business proposition, he could provide and keep a better standard of homes for the Mexican.

The poorly paid laborer can not afford to pay high rent. At present he is unable to rent a decent house in which to live. Surely, Los Angeles, in spite of the high cost of building materials, has enough money to build small houses on her wide areas of uninhabited land. Moreover, certain districts which contain delapidated and tumbled-down shacks should be rebuilt. The garden city plan presents a very possible solution to the problem. Unfortunately, as yet, this plan has not been adapted to suit the needs of the recent immigrant. Expensive apartment houses and palatial homes are springing up with a mushroom growth to house the incoming wealthier class of people. The Mexican is just as much an individual as the Easterner or Northerner. His needs are as much the care of this city as those of her citizens in better financial circumstances. One of the best investments that Los Angeles can make is to build small houses, homes— not merely shelters—for the Mexican. Conditions at present are such that they can be easily handled, but a delay of years means great difficulties.

Looking back over my work among these fifty families and my experience in general with the Mexican, I feel very strongly that action must be taken. The data indicate that the poor housing conditions are not due to any fault of the Mexicans, but rather to the character of the buildings which they may rent and to lack of consideration of the landlords. Improper sanitary arrangements are altogether the fault of the house owner. My personal recommendation is the immediate education of the house-owners. Give them a personal knowledge of the conditions among their tenants. The average landlord is a man, thrifty and busy, careless of human relationships, heedless but not unsympathetic with human suffering. Were he made to feel his responsibility, he would be willing to better conditions. I believe that the housing problem of the Mexican can be solved by the business man.

The data give an accurate statement of the housing conditions among the Mexicans of our district. A few brief sketches have given an insight into the Mexican family itself, but in conclusion I wish to summarize what I believe to be the important points in the present housing situation.

1. The present housing conditions among the Mexicans are not intolerable, but are deplorable and a menace to Los Angeles.

2. Lack of sanitation is the outstanding feature of the current housing situation among the Mexicans.

3. In most cases rents are not high if the houses rented were fit for habitation.

4. At present Los Angeles can not offer the incoming immigrant adequate shelter.

5. The crowded conditions and the absence of pleasing environment are a menace to the morals of the Mexican.

6. The tuberculosis prevalent among the Mexicans is due to dark, ill-drained habitations.

7. Satisfactory homes must be provided for the Mexican in order to promote good citizenship. The present shelter is neither conducive to ambition nor independence.

8. The young Mexican needs a home rather than a shelter, otherwise he will lose the filial affection characteristic of his race.

9. The recent immigrant lacks initiative in the improvement of his home. It is the prerogative of the house-owner to keep his tenant up to a certain standard of cleanliness and maintenance.

10. Education of the house owner concerning the poor housing condition is necessary for immediate improvement.

11. Los Angeles has it within her power to eradicate a growing evil. If she neglects this opportunity of "building for the future," her history will be that of any large city poisoned with slums.

THE NEAR SIDE OF THE
MEXICAN QUESTION

JAY S. STOWELL, M.A.

THE NEAR SIDE OF THE
MEXICAN QUESTION

BY

JAY S. STOWELL, M.A.

NEW YORK
GEORGE H. DORAN COMPANY

TO MY WIFE
ANNE WILDER STOWELL

FOREWORD

There are two sides to nearly every matter and the ever-present Mexican question offers no exception to this general rule. The side of this question of which we hear least is that lying north of the international line, yet this aspect of the situation is of vital concern to every citizen in the United States. The future of our country is unalterably and inextricably bound up with the future of Mexico and the Mexicans. Every passing year but adds emphasis to this fact. The multitude of Mexicans, who have found refuge within our borders during the last decade, added to the not inconsiderable Spanish-American element resident for a much longer period here, forms a group which has become well-nigh indispensable to our national life and one with which we must reckon in the days to come.

It is to help the reader understand something of the intimacy of our relationship to Mexico and the large contribution which Mexicans and Spanish-Americans are already making to our national life that this book is written. If it helps at all toward a sympathetic approach to the common problems which Mexicans and Americans must work out side by side. in the days ahead, it will have accomplished its purpose.

Jay S. Stowell.

New York City.

CONTENTS

THE NEAR SIDE OF THE
MEXICAN QUESTION

THE NEAR SIDE OF THE
MEXICAN QUESTION

CHAPTER I

THE "BORDER"

AN Arizona boy was recently taken by his mother for his first visit to the "Border." He stood at the international line and gazed in every direction. Then in disappointment he turned to his parent and cried, "Why, Mother, I don't see any Border."

The scenery on one side of the line was not particularly different from that on the other; the vegetation was the same; the little adobe huts on the American side looked exactly like those on the Mexican side; and the people were as dark-skinned on one side of the line as on the other. There was a barbed wire fence, to be sure, but it was not labeled, and it was not strikingly different from the thousands of miles of similar fence which crisscross the United States from coast to coast.

No, it was not specially surprising that the boy was disappointed. Our 1,833 miles of Mexican Border have little that is spectacular to offer the visitor. The Rio Grande River which flows between Texas and Mexico is, at certain places and at certain seasons, an imposing stream, but at other points and other seasons it is far

13

from awe-inspiring. Even when it is too deep to be forded, railroad bridges, foot bridges, licensed ferries, and unlicensed boatmen at out-of-the-way points convert the Rio Grande into the stream that unites Texas with Mexico rather than separates her from Mexico. West of El Paso, however, there is no Rio Grande and the Border stretches for hundreds of miles to San Diego and Tia Juana, marked here and there by concrete posts and intermittent stretches of wire fence, but elsewhere unmarked and often unguarded. The thing which impresses the traveler from Brownsville on the east to San Diego on the west is the same thing which impressed the boy, namely, that there is no Border. For nearly two thousand miles the United States stands joined to Mexico. Legally there may be a place where one nation stops and another begins; an instant when you are in the United States and the next instant in Mexico; but such distinctions are artificial, and so far as our Southwestern Border is concerned they can easily be over-emphasized. Human nature has ever ignored artificial barriers, and human nature on the Border is no exception. Life on the two sides of the Border has blended to a remarkable degree.

American business men reside in the United States and spend most of their waking hours in Mexico; Mexican children sleep in Old Mexico and come into the United States each morning to attend school; American laborers work across the line in Mexico and Mexican laborers do every conceivable sort of work in the United States; Mexican women purchase their groceries in the United States and thousands of American women and men go into Mexico to trade, to see the sights and, until recently, at least, to gamble, to play the races, and to otherwise disport themselves; ministers on Sunday preach the Gospel in the United States in the morning, in Old Mexico in the afternoon, and again in the United States at night; railroad and street car passengers get on trains in the United States and ride down into Mexico, and other passengers get on trains in Mexico and ride across into the United States; Mexican criminals seek haven in the United States, and our criminals flee into Mexico. And thus the list might be indefinitely continued. There are important border towns in the United States which are eighty-five per cent Mexican, and where Spanish is the language of the home, the street and the market-place, and there are Mexican towns across the line where English is practically as current as Spanish.

Added to these intimate and inevitable contacts there is the bond of a large and ever-increasing international trade. In spite of internal turmoil in Mexico this has amounted to a large total in recent years. For the fiscal year 1910 just before the resignation of President Diaz it was $115,000,000. In 1917 the total was $191,000,000; in 1918 $245,000,000; in 1919 $278,000,000; and for 1920 it is reported as over $300,000,000. Some one has pointed out that our sales to the 15,000,000 people of Mexico are more than our sales to the 400,000,000 people of China or the 300,000,000 people of India. We import sisal, petroleum, cotton, hides, copper, chick-peas, coffee, mahogany, india rubber, silver and multitudinous other products. In return we send Mexico quantities of manufactured articles and refined products. Before the war we were supplying about one-half of Mexico's imports. It is said that we are now supplying eighty-five per cent of her imports and taking ninety per cent of her exports. Much of the trade which comes directly across the Border passes through Texas, but for the year ending June 30th,

1919, the total imports and exports for the Arizona District were nearly $38,000,000 and for the Southern California District nearly $20,000,000. Douglas and Nogales, Arizona, and Calexico, California, have, within a few years, become very important ports of entry. The large investments of American capital in Mexico have been an important factor in turning Mexican trade to the United States. Before the war the investment of American capital in Mexico was estimated at over $1,000,000,000. It was recently estimated by United States Senator Fall at $2,000,000,000. The War which shut off other sources of supply from Mexico has perhaps been the chief factor in the recent rapid growth of our trade with Mexico.

Now that the War is over the important question arises whether we are to hold the trade which we acquired by force of circumstances while it was in progress. The attitude of the new government in Mexico toward the United States becomes a matter of immediate concern to many an American business man.

To many the term "Mexico" is but a synonym for "revolution," and it is true that during the last decade there have been several overturns in governmental authority. Even before that period Mexico was not a stranger to wars, internal dissensions, and revolutions. Before the coming of the Spaniards under Cortes in 1519 the story of Mexico was the story of the struggle of one group for supremacy over another. By 1376 the power of the Aztecs was generally recognized, and they were the rulers when Cortes appeared. Cortes had been in Mexico City only a month, however, until he had Montezuma II, the last ruler of the Aztecs and Emperor of Mexico, in jail. History tells us that the reign of Montezuma II was occupied "with expeditions of conquest, suppression of revolts, erection of temples, and extensive immolations of human victims." From 1519 until 1821 Mexico was under the direct rule of Spain, exercised during the first fifteen years through military governors and then through Viceroys, of whom there were more than sixty. Some of these were good rulers and some were bad, but in general, with the exception of numerous Indian revolts, they kept the people in subjection, and there was considerable progress in education, mining, agriculture, drainage, commerce and similar lines.

On September 16, 1810, there began the struggle for Mexican independence which lasted for more than a decade, and on October 4, 1824, the first constitution of the Republic of Mexico was proclaimed. There followed a half century of internal dissension, during which revolution followed revolution and Mexican affairs were in continual turmoil until the coming of Porfirio Diaz. During this period the independence of Texas was won (1836) and ten years later the war between Mexico and the United States broke out. This resulted in a new and largely modified boundary for Mexico. In 1876 Diaz assumed control of Mexico and the following year he was elected President of the Republic. From 1876 until 1911 Porfirio Diaz was the dominant figure in Mexico. He established a stable government; negotiated foreign treaties; extended educational facilities; established the credit of Mexico; built railroads, harbor facilities, and other public improvements; and did much to regulate the internal affairs of the Republic. In 1911 Francisco Madero overthrew the power of Diaz and was elected President. Revolts at once broke out and guerrilla warfare sprang up. In 1913 Madero was forced out of the Presidency and four days later was murdered. General Victoriana Huerta assumed control, and his power as provisional President was continued until July 5th, 1914. On August 20th, 1914, Venustiano Carranza made his triumphal entry into Mexico City. He was soon forced out of the City, however. He then set up his government at Puebla and later at Vera Cruz. In one way or another Carranza continued to be the dominant factor in Mexican politics, until the outbreak of the revolution in Sonora, April 10th, 1920. Just thirty days from the outbreak of this revolution Associated Press dispatches told of the flight of President Carranza from the City of Mexico, and on May 22nd press dispatches were telling of the death of Carranza at the hands of his own troops. Adolfo de la Huerta, Governor of the State of Sonora, was made provisional President of the Republic, with General Alvaro Obregon a strong factor in the new government and candidate for the position of President. On September 5th, 1920, General Obregon was elected President.

From such a background, optimism concerning the immediate future of Mexico and of our relations with Mexico can arise either because "hope springs eternal in the human breast" or because there are real reasons for optimism. Probably both factors are at work in the present situation. At any rate there is a surprising amount of optimism along the Border in regard to the future of conditions in Mexico. It chanced that during the entire time that the revolution was in progress I was on the Border and had an opportunity to see the Border phases of it in process. There was little that was spectacular, but there was much that was interesting. Most interesting of all was the conversation of those who were witnessing at short range or were sharing in the revolution in some way. I was over in Carranza's territory and also over in the revolutionists' territory while the revolution was in progress; I talked with officials of both sides; and I talked with many Americans of many sorts, some of whom had lost heavily through the long continued unsettled conditions in Mexico. Not once did I hear the revolution referred to as "another Mexican revolution" or in any other disparaging terms. There was a disposition everywhere to take the movement seriously and to welcome it as a step toward the establishment of a stable and dependable government in Mexico.

So far as the revolution itself was concerned it was conducted with a minimum of violence and bloodshed. In Sonora the revolution caused little disturbance, owing to the fact that the leader of the revolution was the Governor of the State. There was little or no interruption of business across the border, and a visitor to Nogales or to any of the other Arizona points on the Border would have seen nothing to indicate that a revolution was in progress. In Chihuahua General Emilio Salinas, brother-in-law of Carranza and provisional Governor of the State, was imprisoned, but later allowed to escape upon payment of 12,000 pesos. I met General Salinas a few hours after his escape and traveled with him and his young wife for nearly twenty-four hours. He had formerly been Mexican Consul in New York City.

Perhaps the severest disturbance on the Border occurred at Nuevo Laredo just across from Laredo, Texas, on May 9th. General Reynaldo Garza, the Carranza leader, refused to surrender the town. His garrison consisted of sixty men. The revolutionists attacked him with eighty men. The battle lasted for thirty minutes, during which the residents of Laredo gathered at the bank of the river just across from Nuevo Laredo. A few aeroplanes added to the picturesqueness of the situation, and several Mexican women provided the finishing touch by calmly sweeping their sidewalks or patios while the fighting was at its height. Other citizens in Nuevo Laredo watched the fighting from their homes. Almost none of them tried to find refuge in the United States as they had done in previous times of disturbance. General Garza fought for a time, and then he and his son jumped into an automobile and started out in a southeastern direction. The machine was soon punctured by bullets, and the fugitives abandoned it and soon after crossed the Rio Grande into the United States, the desired haven of every hard pressed soul in Mexico. During the fight rifles and automatic pistols were the principal weapons used. The attack occurred at 5:50 o'clock Sunday morning and by 7 o'clock a parade of revolutionists, headed by a band and shouting "Viva Obregon," filled the streets. Simultaneously a revolutionist who had taken part in the attack appeared at the river bank and shouted to the Americans across the river: "We have taken the place; come over, boys!" And the bell in the Catholic church at Nuevo Laredo rang out notes of victory. Two hours after the fighting ceased the place was as quiet and orderly as ever. The saloons were kept closed all day, so there was no disturbance from drunkenness. Seven were reported killed by the fighting and seventeen wounded. As soon as the town was captured an acting mayor was appointed, a police force established and the various customs, immigration and post-office positions filled so that the life of the town might proceed unmolested.

At many other places there was no fighting at all and the transfer of authority was made without disturbance of

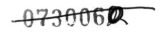

any sort. I stood on the international line at Brownsville while negotiations were being made for turning over the reins of authority in Matamoras just across. There was some slight attempt to check passage across the line until the status of affairs should have been determined and announced, but Mexican women with groceries and other residents had little difficulty in going and coming.

The orderly conduct of the revolution and the evident desire on the part of the leaders to avoid bloodshed were good omens. There is every reason to believe that the revolutionists were as disappointed and grieved over the sad fate which befell Carranza as were his admirers. Of course it was good politics for them to be so, but it is only fair to believe that their motives were humanitarian rather than political. A prominent leader of the revolution told me while Carranza was still in Mexico City that they would be delighted to have him escape, and that they had already offered him safe conduct out of the country if he would avail himself of it. I had at the time, and still have, no reason to doubt his statement. Whether Carranza underestimated the strength of the revolution, or whether he felt that it was undignified for him to flee from the country, he evidently did not care to avail himself of the opportunity to escape.

More significant, however, than the method of conducting the revolution is the attitude of the present leaders of Mexico toward the United States and toward the important questions concerning which Mexico must adopt very definite policies. It is significant that the revolution started in Sonora, a state which has kept on the most friendly relations with the United States, which for years has kept its borders free from the vice on which other Mexican states have fattened, and which has given diligent attention to the building up of wholesome commercial relationships with the United States. Nor have the statements made by the leaders of Mexico since the success of the revolution has been assured been disappointing. Everywhere there has been a new note of sincerity, of integrity of purpose, and of determined friendliness toward the United States. Of course any other attitude would only be folly on Mexico's part and a great disadvantage to the United States. That fact, however, does not minimize the significance of Mexico's frank recognition of it. The leaders of Mexico know that they need the friendly co-operation and assistance of the United States. Possibly it would be a good thing for us if we appreciated a little more clearly how much we need the friendship and confidence of Mexico.

Recently (June 19th, 1920) President de la Huerta gave a dinner to a number of American writers in Mexico City. Some of his remarks are worthy of notice.

Speaking of conditions in Mexico, he said: "I think that the economic situation will soon be better, as I have noted a better atmosphere among bankers and business men, although the men in power are the last to know the true conditions. I may be fooled by this feeling, but it would seem that we are on the road to progress."

When questioned concerning the oil situation, he replied: "We will go half way, and I am sure that the American business interests will come the other half."

He then went on to say that he wished to impress upon the American people that Mexico would be more than friendly, and that he personally would not permit politicians for personal interests to provoke friction. He said that it had been the idea of many Mexican leaders to use fear of the United States as a threat over Mexicans, but that he was determined to use all means in his power to make clear to the United States, by deeds as well as words, that Mexico and the United States should and would be more than friendly.

Since the election of President Obregon he has given voice to some of the ideals and policies which are to dominate his administration. These include an honest government, amnesty for political offenders, punishment of criminals, payment of the national debt, reduction of the army, encouragement of agriculture and business, protection of foreign investments in Mexico, friendship with the United States and other neighbors, development of industry, and other similar items.

Surely those are encouraging sentiments, and we shall get further along the path which leads to properly adjusted relationships with Mexico if, for the present, we accept them at their face value than if we adopt an attitude of suspicion.

In August (1920) General Salvador Alvarado, Minister of Finance for the new government in Mexico, spoke before a group of New York bankers and professional men at the Bankers' Club in New York City. He spoke frankly of the needs of Mexico after a decade of revolution and disorder, but he also spoke encouragingly of the "newly awakened national conscience in Mexico." He said in part:

"The great longing for peace, reorganization, work, and prosperity is equally strong in the banker as in the farmer, the merchant, or the cattle raiser, the skilled worker or the common laborer; all are ready to settle down and work. This enthusiasm, confidence, and optimism are the surest signs that the revolutionary era is over in Mexico, at least so far as the present generation is concerned.

"The new government of Mexico formed mostly of young and progressive men who joined the revolution only because they thought it was their duty to do so, is conscious of the state of mind of the country, as well as of Mexico's duty, if Mexico wants to be considered as a member of the community of civilized nations.

"This government has drafted a vast plan for the reconstruction and reorganization of the country, covering all national activities.

"You may not believe it, but it is nevertheless true that all our trains are running on schedule, that all public services are in normal operation, and our crops this year will be the largest on record. And as to any anti-foreign sentiment, I can assure you that none exists; on the contrary there is probably on the surface of the earth no other people more hospitable and warm-hearted toward foreigners than the Mexicans. I wish to say that before I came to this country I heard also of an intense anti-Mexican feeling prevailing in the United States, but I wish to state that my two visits have completely convinced me that such sentiment does not exist. The same thing is true. about Mexico."

To be sure these are only words, but they are reassuring words both because of the sentiments which they express and of the evident sincerity which is back of them. Up to the time of this writing we have had no reason for refusing to take them at their face value.

When the chairman introduced Señor Alvarado at the gathering mentioned above, he referred half humorously to the fact that he was under no embarrassment in entertaining General Alvarado in spite of the fact that the country had become dry, because the visitor himself had the distinction of being the original prohibitionist of Mexico. He went on to explain that as Governor of Yucatan under Carranza General Alvarado had made that state dry. Yucatan, however, has not been the only dry spot in Mexico, for Sonora at least has been dry, or largely so, for some time. This condition existed under Governor Calles even before de la Huerta became Governor of the State. When Agua Prieta went dry a Chinese evidently did not take the matter seriously. He opened a saloon, but he was in jail before night. A little later saloons at border points were permitted to sell liquor to American visitors. This soon became a nuisance, however, and the saloons of Sonora were tightly closed once more.

Mexico still has a long road to travel before her political and social life can be organized on a genuinely democratic basis. Education must be extended and common ideals inculcated before this can be achieved, but, although no one can foresee what accidents are in store, there is no apparent reason why Mexico should not travel this road with no more than the ordinary misadventures. Although a republic in name, Mexico has really had no experience in self-government until the last ten years, and if she has made a good many mistakes she has also learned a good many lessons which should be of inestimable value in the years ahead. As her neighbor we are profoundly interested both from altruistic and selfish motives in Mexico's welfare.

One of the first matters which confronted the new Mexican government was what to do with Lower California, perhaps the one outstanding area where the revolution did not seem to "take," and a region in which Americans of several sorts had become deeply interested.

While the revolution was still in progress I asked T. R. Beltran, an agent of the revolutionists, "What do you plan to do with Lower California and Governor Cantu?"

He replied, "We will give him a chance to come in, and then if he refuses we shall be obliged to go and compel him to come in."

In line with this policy, the new government very soon sent word to Governor Cantu to come to Mexico City and report. Now for ten years Cantu had not been in the habit of reporting to anybody, and very naturally he did not comply with the demand of the government. For the first time in many years, therefore, an expedition to Lower California was organized; Cantu was ousted from his position of authority; he departed for the United States, and Luis Salazar took control of the "lost state." For ten years the central government of Mexico had been too busy to concern itself with Lower California. During that time Esteban Cantu went on his way unmolested by governmental interference or by revolutionary uprisings. He built up a little private kingdom within a republic, and, naturally, that could not permanently continue. He had a few troubles of his own. At one time considerable dissatisfaction developed among the natives over the important concessions which Cantu granted to foreigners, particularly the Chinese and Japanese. By taking precautions, however, Cantu was able to ward off what seemed like impending trouble, and to continue to do pretty much as he pleased.

Lower California is a mountainous peninsula 750 miles long and from thirty to one hundred and forty miles wide. It forms the most western part of Mexico and comprises an area of 58,343 square miles, or a little more than the area of Wisconsin. It is separated from the rest of Mexico by the Gulf of California, by an almost impassable desert in the western part of Sonora, and by the Colorado River. Much of its area is uninhabited and uninhabitable, but there are some outstanding exceptions along the western coast and the northern border. In 1910 the population was 52,244. It is doubtless considerably larger than that now as the last ten years have witnessed remarkable developments at several points. For some time the capital of Lower California has been located at Ensenada de Todos Santos on the west coast. A fine automobile road runs from here to Tia Juana between the ocean and the mountains, and Tia Juana just across the line from San Diego, California, is connected with San Diego both by trolley and by railroad. Ensenada, Tia Juana, and Mexicali further east, just across from Calexico, California, are the three most important places in Lower California. The interest of Americans is chiefly in the two border points, Tia Juana and Mexicali.

Mexicali on the Mexican side of the line and Calexico on the American side form in reality a single community with a combined population of approximately 16,000, two-thirds of which is on the Mexican side of the line. Of the total population there are perhaps 7,000 Mexicans, 4,000 Chinese (chiefly in Mexicali) and 5,000 of American or mixed stocks. These two towns lie in the heart of the rich Imperial Valley, which has within recent years been transformed by the waters of the Colorado River from one of the most absolute deserts in the world to a veritable garden spot. In 1918 the assessed valuation of the irrigated land in this region was approximately $36,000,-000; the same year the value of the farm products was $50,000,000. In 1910 there were only 793 people in

Calexico, and 650 in Mexicali. A very large import and export trade with Mexico has sprung up at this point. In 1918 this totaled $9,521,000, as compared with $7,877,000 for the five other ports of the District of Southern California, including Los Angeles and San Diego.

Cotton is one of the chief products of this section, particularly on the Mexican side, where Chinese, who have been granted important concessions by Governor Cantu, are raising thousands of acres of cotton. Large cotton gins are located at Mexicali. The Chinese who work here have come, many of them, through the United States, and it is a not uncommon sight to see a carload of new recruits, landed at some American port, but destined for Lower California, passing through to Mexico in a locked car with heavily barred windows.

The water which renders productive the land on the Mexican side of the Border is from the same source as that which is used for a similar purpose on the American side. It comes from the Colorado River, but it passes down through a portion of Mexico before it returns to water the Imperial Valley in the United States. This fact has given rise to many conjectures as to what might happen if we were to get into difficulty with Mexico, and has led to extended discussions in Congress concerning the possibility of an "all-American ditch." Those who were watching this project some years ago will remember how the river broke bounds, and for nearly two years poured its water down into the Valley, forming the now famous Salton Sea and threatening to inundate the entire region. President Roosevelt's appeal to Congress for help was unheeded, and the Southern Pacific Railroad, under the direction of Mr. Harriman, finally closed the gap, although it involved running trains of new steel cars loaded with rocks and dumping them, cars and all, into the break. All of this expense was later charged back against the land in the Valley.

Governor Cantu had, however, other sources of revenue than legitimate business, and he waxed fat under his various revenues, particularly from commercialized vice. A count in Mexicali, while he was in control, showed ten pool rooms, twenty-one saloons, two Chinese gambling houses with lotteries, one bull ring, and a theatre, gambling house, bar and house of prostitution combined. This latter institution, which was owned and operated by three Americans and was directly controlled and managed by one of them, occupied the most conspicuous square in the center of town. It was said to pay $22,000 per month into Governor Cantu's pocket as a license fee and to have had a total overhead expense of $40,000 per month. The 150 American, Negro, and Mexican women housed here paid a monthly license fee said to be $27.50 each, a daily rental of two dollars each, and an inspection fee of two dollars per week. The principal owner of this institution is commonly rated as a millionaire, and one of his reported stock remarks was, "Every man in the Imperial Valley is working for me." During the War this institution took $70,000 worth of Liberty Bonds at one time.

The other great center of vice in Lower California was Tia Juana. Here a race track and multitudinous other institutions attracted regularly thousands of visitors who either liked the excitement of a place where the "lid was off" or who were seeking to earn a living by some questionable method. Transportation was made easy by railroad, bus, and electric car service from San Diego. The whole situation was demoralizing, both locally and nationally.

One of the finest things which the new government in Mexico has done is to clean up the resorts both here and at Mexicali, and to declare its policy of establishing a "dry zone" along the Border. Under the conditions which have been permitted to exist along the Border it was hard for Mexico to develop any feeling of respect for America and Americans, and in the same way Mexico's reputation suffered among Americans because of the unfavorable impression which the Border presented of conditions in Mexico. The entire situation was against the development of those wholesome relations between the two sides of the Border which should exist, if our mutual business, social, and political interests are to be cared for and a firm foundation laid for future prosperity.

The United States has perhaps been equally responsible with Mexico for the unfortunate conditions which have existed at so many points along the Border, for we have many times furnished both the capital and the patronage which has made vice profitable. At any rate, we may all rejoice at what seems like the dawning of a better day with a less murky atmosphere for our Mexican Border. We have a chance here to help Mexico maintain the standards which she has set up. It is significant and not particularly to our credit that, when President de la Huerta tried for the first time to limit the sale of liquor in Mexico City, the American press reported that the Mexicans took the decision without protest, while Americans in the City made vigorous protestations against this interference with their "rights."

So far as the United States is concerned, the Mexican problem is inescapable. It is to our direct advantage to see Mexico prosper in every way. Our relations with her must be placed upon the sure foundations of morality, integrity, and Christian neighborliness. Everything that makes for the establishment of those conditions we may well encourage. Mexico has passed through some difficult days and, before these words are read, some dissension in her government may threaten her peace, but in spite of misadventures there is every reason to believe that the leaders and the common people of Mexico are tired of turmoil, and that with our help they stand ready to work out an altogether new future for themselves. Whether this be true or not, it is true that the expulsive power of the recent revolutions in Mexico has placed the Mexican in a position to build himself into the future of our own country in quite a new way. Without much ado he has gone at the job, and the indications are that he will "make good" at it.

CHAPTER II

THE MEXICAN AT WORK IN THE UNITED STATES

THE emigration of Mexicans to the United States began something over three hundred years ago. There is no record that the stream has ever stopped, but it is only within the last decade that the tiny rivulet has swelled to proportions sufficient to attract attention. Since 1911, however, every overturn of the political craft in Mexico has been followed by the eager scramble of a certain proportion of the survivors to find refuge in the United States. Some of these newcomers have been political refugees who have suddenly discovered that the climate of the United States was far more healthful and salubrious than the climate of Mexico, but multitudes of others have been simple Mexican peons, who, for one reason or another, have found life intolerable in Old Mexico, and have been attracted by the superior economic and educational opportunities which the United States seemed to offer.

The wealthier refugees have settled in many centers from Los Angeles, El Paso, San Antonio, Laredo and other Border towns to New York and other eastern cities. The poor Mexican has for lack of means usually been forced to make his first stand at some point close to the Border. Later, as opportunities have offered, he has found his way to more distant regions.

We already had a large Spanish-speaking element with Mexican affiliations and of Mexican extraction in our themselves not only in the Southwest, but from the Pacific Coast through to our eastern states. On January 13th, 1920, the Santa Fe Railroad reported as employed on its Western Lines in the states of Kansas, Colorado, New Mexico, Texas, and Oklahoma 6,077 Mexicans. A large proportion of these men were employed on track work, but some were engaged in cleaning cinder pits, wiping engines, cleaning cars, icing cars, loading stock and similar occupations. Others were reported working as machinists and boilermakers, and engaged in similar occupations in the mechanical department. At about the same time there were reported on the Eastern Lines of the same railroad approximately 4,200 Mexicans. About ten per cent of this number were employed in the mechanical department in shops and roundhouses and the remainder principally on track work. This division covers part of Kansas and Oklahoma as well as Missouri and Illinois. On the Coast Lines of the Santa Fe there were employed about 4,000 Mexicans. Thus on this one railroad something over 14,000 Mexicans were employed. The manager of the Western Lines says of their record as laborers, "While not as energetic or competent as white men, they are as a rule satisfactory for track work and other work of that nature, and probably more so than other alien labor which can be secured for this purpose."

On the Pennsylvania railroad Mexicans have been employed in limited numbers at various points between New York and Pittsburgh and Buffalo. The General Manager of the Eastern Lines of this railroad says of their work, "As a class they were among the best track laborers of any foreign nationality." Numerous other railroads, particularly in the West and the Southwest, are largely dependent upon Mexican labor.

220,000 Spanish-Americans. A man who has studied the situation in Arizona for years says that there are more than 100,000 in Arizona, and the Spanish-speaking population of California has recently been estimated as approaching 250,000. Whatever the exact numbers may be, their name is "legion," and they are to be found not only in our Border states but by thousands in Colorado, Nevada, Idaho, Kansas, Oklahoma, Indiana, Illinois, Pennsylvania, Michigan, New York, New England and in many other states both east and west. The largest single colony in the United States is perhaps at San Antonio, Texas, which is said to have a Mexican population of 50,000. El Paso, Texas, is reported fifty-five per cent Mexican, and Los Angeles, California, has a Mexican population of 30,000.

During the War the shortage of common labor in the Southwest led to the admission under special permit of otherwise inadmissible aliens. Since the war this custom has been continued, and three clauses of the immigration law have for the purpose been suspended, namely, the literacy test, the head tax, and the contract labor clauses. Under this special provision thousands of Mexican laborers have been admitted to the United States. A very careful record with a photograph of each immigrant thus admitted is kept and the employer becomes responsible for the return of the immigrant. In case there is trouble, deportation may take place at the employer's expense. Owing to the admission of these laborers, vast areas of irrigated land which would otherwise have remained untilled have been producing bountiful crops.

Mexicans in the United States have distinguished themselves in a number of fields of labor. Thus on the railroads of our country they have made a large place for country, particularly in the Southwest. Although the traditions and environment of Spanish-Americans and Mexicans are quite different in many respects, yet in others they are almost identical. The mere fact that they speak a common language helps to blend the two elements into one common group. Just how large this group is, it is not easy to state. It is frankly admitted by immigration officials that many of these newcomers have entered the United States over unauthorized paths, and no record has, therefore, been kept of them. The limited appropriations for the Immigration Bureau have made an adequate Border patrol impossible. Possibly the zeal of officials has also been dampened by the fact that farmers and ranchers in the Border states have been very glad to welcome Mexican laborers regardless of the path by which they may have arrived. Once in the United States they form a constantly shifting group very difficult to enumerate, and totals are further complicated by the fact that thousands of Spanish-Americans are, for census purposes, "Americans of American parentage." In view of the fact that the Mexican is legally a "white" man, his totals do not apppear in any race grouping based on the color of the skin.

The best estimate available at the present writing indicates that there are approximately 1,500,000 Mexicans and Spanish-Americans in the United States at present. Texas has the largest group of any of the states, and recent estimates indicate that her total population of Mexicans and Spanish-Americans approximates 450,000. The Secretary of State's office in New Mexico estimates that the state is at least sixty per cent Spanish-American. This would give a total for New Mexico of approximately

In the growing of sugar beets the Mexican has become next to indispensable. The new and rapidly developing beet sugar industry of the United States could never have made the enormous strides which it has made in recent years had it not been for Mexican assistance. You may travel from the far western beet fields of Southern California to the northern areas of Idaho or the eastern beet sections of Michigan and everywhere you will find Mexicans working patiently and efficiently in the beet fields, driving the heavy wagons loaded with beets and assisting about the beet sugar factories. It was largely to increase the production of sugar beets that the special arrangement for the admission of contract labor from Mexico was made. The raising of sugar beets is of course a seasonal occupation, and the introduction of Mexican labor into the beet fields has brought with it some of the problems which come with seasonal employment. A newspaper item dated October 27, 1919, at Pocatello, Idaho, tells of the difficulty which Idaho faces with several thousand Mexicans on hand and nothing for them to do after the beet season is over, and then quotes the local federal immigration inspector as follows:

"I'll be hanged if I know what to think of it, or what to do about it. We need these Mexican laborers at certain seasons of the year to do work that American laborers will not do. They are needed and needed badly to cultivate the beets and to harvest them. They were brought here under a special agreement with the labor department in 1918 to save the sugar beet crop. It was agreed that they were to have the same wages paid to other laborers, and this looked big to them. But their work only lasts a few weeks in the early summer and another few weeks in the late fall. They begin weeding beets in the latter part of May or June 1st, and when beet harvest comes on they have worked up to about the middle of November. What are they to do between these periods? They cannot earn enough to live a year on these few weeks' work."

Similar situations exist in Colorado, Wyoming, Utah, Iowa, Nebraska, and other states, but that does not change the fact that the Mexican has made a large place for himself in the sugar beet industry which is to-day supplying millions of pounds of sugar for domestic consumption in the United States.

In Southern California the Mexican does not, however, confine his activities to the sugar beet industry. He may be seen working in the orange orchards, helping in the large groves of English walnut trees, or dominating the lima bean enterprise of the immense "lima bean empire" of that rich state. In fact, there is hardly a fruit or a vegetable of any sort in California in the production or distribution of which the Mexican is not having a part. Around Los Angeles and other centers Mexicans have recently been employed in the raising of flowers for the floral trade, and it has been discovered that they are exceptionally well adapted to this fine art.

In this connection a prominent florist of California says:

"Mexicans are coming to be the finest florists that we can secure. The Japanese and Belgians, both specifically trained in their countries to do this work, are not as good as the Mexicans. Several nurseries and florists, that I know of, are turning off their Japanese and other employees and are taking on Mexicans."

In many states of the West, such as Arizona, New Mexico, Texas, Colorado and the states farther north,

Mexican cowboys care for uncounted thousands of cattle; and Mexican herders tend multitudes of sheep. The loneliness of this latter occupation has few terrors for the Mexican, and he will uncomplainingly take his sheep out into the wilderness and care for them alone when other workmen will refuse to undertake the task. Thus the Mexican is having a large part in the production of the wool for our clothing, the leather for our shoes and the beef for the nourishment of our bodies.

At mining the Mexican is particularly skillful. An American who has for many years been mining with Mexicans describes them as "natural miners." In coal, copper, gold, silver, and many other sorts of mining projects in the West and Southwest the Mexican is playing an important part.

Possibly no single state has profited so generously from Mexican labor as has Texas. This state is now at the very head of the procession of agricultural states, and the thing which has made this rapid advance possible has been Mexican labor. In 1919 Texas ranked third among the states in the production of corn, with 202,800,000 bushels to her credit. At the same time Texas produced 2,700,000 bales of cotton, or more than one-fifth of the total national crop. And Texas realizes her indebtedness to the Mexican. John B. Carrington, Secretary of the San Antonio Chamber of Commerce, is quoted by Gerald B. Breitigam as saying in this connection:

"We couldn't do it if we didn't have the labor. Yes, sir, we are dependent upon the Mexican farm labor supply and we know it. Mexican farm labor is rapidly proving the making of this state."

In many places in Texas the Mexican has entirely displaced the Negro or made his services unnecessary, and his activities in agriculture are not limited to any one crop. Recently a town in Southern Texas announced that for the 1920 season it had already shipped 1,058 carloads of Bermuda onions, and the season was only partly over. Practically all of these onions were produced by Mexican labor. In a similar way the Mexican shared in the production of Texas' many other crops. Surely these facts are of national significance at a time when foodstuffs are well-nigh prohibitive in price.

Possibly one of the most interesting projects dependent upon Mexican labor in the United States is to be found in the Salt River Valley of Arizona. A few years ago this valley was as utter and absolute a desert as could be found in any part of the United States; to-day there are few places more productive. The backbone of this project is the Roosevelt Dam and the water for irrigation which it supplies. This dam, begun September 20, 1906, and completed February 5, 1911, is 284 feet high. It not only supplies the water which is fed out to the thirsty land in the valley through some 800 miles of main canals, but it also is the means of creating thousands of horsepower of electric current. This current is used, among other things, to pump still more water from wells in the valley, so that altogether there are 300,000 acres of irrigated land in the valley. It is predicted that by 1921 this area will be increased to 400,000 acres. On these acres many crops are grown, including alfalfa, cotton, barley, corn, wheat, oats, sorghum, cantaloupes, oranges, grapefruit, olives, apricots, peaches, Irish potatoes, sweet potatoes, lettuce, beans, and small fruit. For some years cotton has been the largest single crop. In 1917 16,200 bales were raised, in 1918 there were 34,000 bales and in 1919

60,000 bales. In 1919 more than 90,000 acres of land were devoted to the raising of cotton here; in 1920 this acreage had increased to nearly 150,000 acres, and the yield will be proportionately enlarged. The cotton grown here is known as "Pima" cotton. It is a sport developed from Egyptian cotton introduced by the United States government for experimental purposes. The fiber is unusually long and fine, with the result that this cotton is eagerly sought after for making the fabric of automobile tires, aeroplane and balloon materials, and mercerized goods. Automobile tire concerns have already invested millions of dollars in the growing of cotton in this Valley. In February, 1920, this cotton sold as high as 97½ cents per pound. The cotton crop for the season 1919-1920 was valued at $20,000,000 and the total products for the valley at $45,000,000. The other shipments included 200 carloads of lettuce, 1,900 carloads of cantaloupes and many other things.

The significant fact for our present purposes, however, is that millions of dollars of invested capital are here dependent for their productiveness upon Mexican labor. Added to the Spanish-speaking laborers already available, thousands of contract laborers have been shipped into this region. During the winter of 1919-1920 4,000 of these workers were retained throughout the winter, lest the same conditions of return might not be permitted during the spring of 1920. It developed that the special plan for admitting laborers was continued, but there was work on roads and construction projects sufficient during the winter to keep the thousands who were retained busy, so there was no loss. In fact, it was felt that it would be worth while to feed these Mexicans during the winter at the expense of the growers rather than to run the risk of losing their assistance the following year, for as one grower employing forty-five families of Mexicans said, "We would go bankrupt at once without the Mexicans."

The list of occupations in which Mexicans are to be found in increasing numbers is almost limitless. There are Mexican storekeepers, laundrymen, barbers, clerks, chauffeurs, printers, streetsweepers, newsvenders, bootblacks, window-cleaners, gardeners, cobblers, expressmen, meat-cutters, scrub-women, factory workers, ranchers, teamsters, carpenters, plumbers, and many others. Nor does this complete the list. One of the leading, if not the leading surgeon in a large Southwestern city is a Mexican Indian. A recent Governor of a Southwestern state is a Mexican by birth and an American by adoption. There are Mexican or Mex-American judges, state legislators, lawyers, ministers, social workers, court reporters and teachers. It is perhaps fair to say that there is not an individual in the United States who is not directly or indirectly indebted to the Mexicans who have crossed the Border and who are at work in the United States. Surely every one of us would feel the pinch of it if the Mexican should by some mysterious process be suddenly removed from our midst. Proceeding humbly, quietly, and unheralded, he has made himself indispensable to our welfare.

And these Mexicans who do so many different things for us are as a class good workers. One man who had been employing Mexican labor on a large scale for twenty-seven years said in reply to a question relative to his opinion of Mexican labor, "If any one tries to tell you that the Mexican is not a good worker, you may tell him for me that he does not know what he is talking about." Another man employing a large number of Mexicans in the raising of cotton was asked what he thought of Mexican labor and why he did not endeavor to get Negro help. He replied, "The Mexican is a good, faithful worker, always quiet and orderly, and we would not for a moment think of exchanging him for Negro help." Similar testimony comes from many different sources.

The Mexican who comes across the international line to work in the United States does not, however, come alone. He brings his wife and family with him. This is true Mexican custom, for the Mexican has been accustomed to take his women folks along to provide food, even when he has been serving in the army. It is quite different from the custom of immigrants from many other countries. Possibly the nearness of Mexico to the United States and the ease with which the journey across the line can be made have something to do with the matter. On a recent visit to an immigration office on the Border, a card picked at random from the files showed that the Mexican whose record it contained had brought with him a wife and nine children into the United States. This instance is more or less typical, for the Mexican families are large. A group of Mexican laborers, therefore, means at once a new Mexican settlement in the United States or an old one enlarged, and since an overwhelming proportion of the Mexicans who come into the country are very poor various social problems are more or less inevitable in every Mexican colony.

When the average Mexican immigrant arrives he brings little or nothing with him except the clothes on his back, yet what he brings represents his entire earthly possessions. He finds himself a stranger in a strange land, the language of which he does not understand. Of course the fact that many of his fellow-countrymen have preceded him helps him at this point as at others. He moves into the cheapest shack which he can find, or he shares the already overcrowded space allotted to a previously arriving immigrant. One case of this kind which came to the writer's attention recently was that of a family of eleven living in one room, the use of which was donated free by a poor Mexican woman whose heart was touched by the need of a fellow-Mexican. Even when a place of abode is found the difficulties of the newcomer are not ended. Unless he is a contract laborer brought in by an employer who immediately needs his services, he must at once find employment in order to supply the necessities of life to himself and his family. If he is in the city, he may go to an employment office conducted by some church or other social agency, and there be told of a place where help is needed. He takes the address and starts out, but his timidity, his ignorance of the English language, and his general inexperience make it impossible for him to find the place toward which he is supposed to be bound. This circumstance happens often enough to make it a real problem for volunteer employment agencies which are endeavoring to be of service to the Mexican immigrant. Thus in many ways the path of the newly-arrived Mexican in the United States is far from a rosy one. If perchance the situation is complicated by sickness in the family or of the bread-winner himself, the entire family is at once reduced to desperate straits.

The houses which the Mexican finds available for his occupancy when he arrives are for the most part small adobe huts or wooden shacks. Now, it must not be thought that adobe in itself is necessarily an inferior building material for use in a dry climate, for some of the best buildings in the Southwest are of adobe construction, but a one-room adobe hut with a dirt floor is a no more suitable place for establishing a home than is a wooden shack under the same conditions. When the number of rooms is increased to two, or three, or four, the situation is of course by that much improved. Tens of thousands of these little homes occupied by Mexicans and Spanish-Americans may be seen scattered throughout the Southwest. In the cities the situation is often not materially different, except that congestion tends to be increased both as to the houses themselves and as to the number of individuals living in a particular house. Here the house court, the remodeled residence, and the shack rented at exorbitant rentals abound. A recent study of the housing situation among Mexicans in Los Angeles showed that one per cent of the families lived in one-room houses, two per cent in two-room houses, twenty-four per cent in three-room houses, thirty per cent in four-room houses, and twenty per cent in five-room houses. This condition represented an improvement over the situation revealed by a survey in 1912 when eighteen per cent of the people were reported as living in one-room houses and sixty per cent in two-room houses. In spite of improvement, housing conditions in the Mexican quarter of Los Angeles are very bad and they are perhaps fairly typical of conditions to be found in other congested city centers where Mexicans are dwelling. In Los Angeles twenty-eight per cent of the habitations studied had no sinks, thirty-two per cent had no lavatories in the houses, and seventy-nine per cent had no baths. Of these houses only five per cent were classed by the Housing Commission as good; more than half were rated as poor or very bad. In spite of unsatisfactory conditions, rents have been rapidly advanced until the housing problem has become a serious one for the Mexican in more aspects than one. The food of the Mexican is on the same unsatisfactory level as are his housing conditions. Often this is due to dire poverty; possibly more often to ignorance concerning the simplest facts related to an adequate diet. Everywhere throughout the Southwest the Mexican is a steady and consistent consumer of beans. Beans form the staple article of diet, and, under unfortunate conditions, the only article. Under better conditions the beans are supplemented by tortillas, coffee, chili, and meat when it can be secured. Owing to the warm climate, flies and other unsanitary conditions, even this is not always wholesome. Unfortunately the Mexican in the United States appears to consume very few dairy products. He uses very little milk, no butter, and only a small amount of cheese. There is reason to believe that much of the sickness among the Mexicans and the apparent lack of energy at times is due to insufficient nourishment. Social workers tell of sick babies covered with sores made well in a short space of time merely by changing the diet from beans to milk, and boarding-school superintendents tell of remarkable physical transformations on the part of pupils with an accompanying rebirth of animal spirits merely by the change from the home food to the more adequate diet of the school dining-room. One of the outstanding needs of the Mexican in the Southwest is some definite instruction in food values and some training in the preparation of foodstuffs. To some extent the schools are beginning to render a real ministry at this point among the boys and girls, but as yet only a beginning has been made. As to the matter of actual relief some social centers already give out milk daily to children and to tuberculosis sufferers and others.

Naturally the entire question of health is closely bound up with that of food and housing. It is not to be expected that, with unsatisfactory and unsanitary houses and with poor and inadequate food, the health of Mexicans will be of the best. As a matter of fact, disease is prevalent and the death rate is high. Thus in Los Angeles it was discovered that while the rate of infant mortality for the City as a whole was 54 to 1,000, the rate for Mexican babies was 152 to 1,000. In other words, a Mexican baby born in Los Angeles has just one-third the chance to survive as has the average baby for the entire city. Of the total deaths for the City of Los Angeles for the year 1918-1919 11.1 per cent were deaths of Mexicans, although the Mexican population of the city was only five per cent of the total population. Tuberculosis is one of the prevalent diseases, and a tuberculosis map of Los Angeles coincides in important details to a map showing the Mexican residence section of the city. The causes given for these unsatisfactory health conditions are the low wage, poor and insufficient food, overcrowding and lack of ventilation, lack of facilities for cleanliness, ignorance in regard to personal hygiene, and the prevalence of flies. In other sections of the Southwest social diseases are prevalent and much suffering is caused by them.

The entire question of wages has a large bearing upon living conditions. The Los Angeles study showed that seventy-two per cent of all the Mexicans employed in the city were working as laborers; fourteen per cent were listed as skilled workers; seven per cent as in the professions; and five per cent were reported as unemployed. Before the war daily wages were as low as $1.60. More recent studies show the average wage of the Mexican laborer in Los Angeles as $3.45 per day. Inquiries in different parts of the Southwest would seem to indicate that daily wages for laborers varied from approximately $2.50 to $4.00. Sheep herders are paid in certain sections from $90 to $110 per month and other ranch labor is secured for less than that amount. In the mild climate of many parts of the Southwest wages go farther than they would in a more rigorous climate, but it should also be remembered that employment is by no means constant, and that often the earnings of a few weeks must be made to stretch over much longer periods or else seasons of want soon follow those of plenty for the Mexican household. The fact that so many of the Mexicans in the United States are poor does not by any means necessarily imply that they are by nature improvident. It often simply registers an income inadequate to cover the needs of a large and growing family. Some means of giving more constant employment to seasonal labor must be worked out before the Mexican will have a fair economic chance at life. In spite of untoward conditions, however, our entire Southwest is dotted with little homes of many sorts, purchased, paid for and owned by Mexicans and Spanish-Americans.

For the most part there has been little organized discontent on the part of Mexican laborers in the United States, although agitators and propagandists of many sorts have been at work among them. It was recently reported that the I. W. W. headquarters in Chicago had three Mexican and Spanish editors busily engaged in preparing and sending out inflammatory literature to the Southwest and into other important Spanish-speaking centers. The very ignorance of the Mexican furnishes a fertile field for this sort of propaganda, and it is hard to tell what may come of it unless it is counteracted by just and sympathetic treatment, by persistent education, and by an intelligent effort to alleviate unsatisfactory conditions.

For those who have been accustomed to think of the Mexican as somewhat of a bandit or brigand it is not altogether easy to picture him as a timid, quiet, peaceable, polite, and kindly person who will go out of his way to avoid trouble, yet the latter picture is perhaps more accurate than the former so far as the Mexican in the United States is concerned. When trouble does come the Mexican sometimes takes matters into his own hand and inflicts such retribution upon his enemy as he sees fit. This is not particularly surprising when we remember that he has for years been living in a land where orderly processes of law have been far from thoroughly established. Even such conflicts, however, are usually of Mexican with Mexican rather than of Mexican with American. So far as we have the facts, there is every reason to believe that as a peaceful, law-abiding member of the community the Mexican ranks well with the native-born American. Thus in the City of Los Angeles in the year 1919 the percentage of Mexican arrests to the total number of arrests for the entire city was 5.5 per cent in a population which is five per cent Mexican. It is evident that the ratios here were not appreciably different. Of the total arrests 34.9 per cent were for drunkenness. Of the 962 cases of drunkenness, 780 occcurred before July 1st when war-time prohibition went into effect; during June of that year 142 Mexicans were arrested for drunkenness and during July only nineteen. Other offenses charged against Mexicans were violation of traffic regulations, vagrancy, petty larceny, disturbing the peace, and burglary. These were the most numerous violations charged.

On the other hand, twenty-three per cent of all applicants for relief at the County Charities in Los Angeles were Mexicans. Thus one-twentieth of the people furnished practically one-fourth of the charity cases. The causes making for poverty in these cases were reported in order of importance as follows: Acute illness, chronic physical disability, death of bread winner, old age, tuberculosis, desertion, insufficient employment, death in family, non-support, maternity, intemperance, imprisonment, insanity, accident (general), unable to locate, industrial incompetency, blindness, poorly paid employment, feeble minded, accident (industrial). The earnings of men in this poverty group ran as low as $1.25 per day. The Mexican in poverty is more the victim of accident and unfortunate circumstances than of intentional error. Added to that he is at the mercy of every unscrupulous exploiter from the rent gouger and the profiteer in foodstuffs and other necessities of life to the seller of enlarged photographs and useless bric-a-brac. Nothing but the diligent neighborliness of Americans in the communities in which he lives will protect the Mexican from the multitude of enemies and carefully-laid snares which beset his path as he endeavors to establish himself in the new land to which he has come and in whose interests he is laboring so diligently.

CHAPTER III

SPANISH-AMERICANS IN NEW MEXICO

NEW MEXICO, one of our youngest states, is probably more thoroughly dominated by a non-Anglo-Saxon, non-English-speaking citizenry than any other state in the Union. The circumstances which have brought this unique distinction to the state are deeply imbedded in the events of the past, and it is not easy to understand the present situation in this large and increasingly important commmonwealth unless we pause to consider something of its history.

When Cortes and his followers were conquering Mexico as early as 1519 they kept hearing from the natives of a "fair land" to the north, but for the moment their attention was confined to the conquest of that part of "New Spain" which was more distinctly tributary to the present Mexico City. In the year 1527 Panfilo de Narvaez, the Spanish soldier and conquistador, was given a grant authorizing him to explore and to govern all that part of New Spain which extended from Florida westward through all of the territory occupied by our present Gulf States and on to and including the present state of New Mexico, Texas and the northern part of Mexico. This Narvaez expedition started from Spain June 17, 1527. It landed on the coast of Florida and started westward. Misled by Indian guides, entangled in the swamps, suffering from hunger and deprivation, attacked by hostile natives, and finally shipwrecked on hastily constructed boats, the expedition collapsed and Narvaez himself died before New Mexico was reached. Nine years after this expedition started from Spain a few survivors made their way down through Texas and Mexico to Mexico City, where they arrived July 24, 1536. Three years later (1539) friar Marcus de Niza, an Italian missionary who had become a Franciscan monk and had entered the service of Spain, left the City of Mexico to explore the country now included in Arizona and New Mexico. He had with him a Negro, one of the survivors of the ill-fated Narvaez expedition. (Some historians say that survivors of this expedition entered New Mexico under the leadership of De Vaca after the death of Narvaez. Others insist even more strongly that there is no evidence to indicate that any of the Narvaez party reached as far west and north as New Mexico.) It is said that Marcos sent the Negro ahead of him with the instruction that if he discovered a mean thing he was to send a white cross one handful long, if a greater thing a white cross two handfuls long, and if a very great thing a large cross. The story goes on to relate that the Negro kept the natives busy carrying crosses taller than a man back to Marcos. The party reached at least as far as the pueblos of the Zuni Indians. The Negro, however, adopted high-handed methods in dealing with the natives, and he was at last killed by them for appropriating property and women not his own. Friar Marcos returned home with glowing accounts of the country and the things which he had seen.

The following year (1540) Francisco Vasquez Coronado was appointed Governor of the Province of "New Galicia," and he organized an expedition for the conquest of the "Seven Cities of Cibola," which friar Marcos claimed to have discovered. A large force of mounted men, infantry, and natives, well-armed and well-supplied with food, set out for the north. When Coronado reached the Zuni country he sent expeditions both east and west to explore the country. The western expedition went as far as the Grand Canyon and the eastern expedition explored parts of New Mexico. The Zunis were rather anxious to get rid of Coronado so they told him wonderful stories of a rich land farther on toward the east. They gladly furnished a guide and Coronado departed. The country got more and more barren as they progressed, and after long and weary wanderings they hanged their guide, who had at last confessed his deception. The party returned to the Rio Grande River and later to Mexico. Coronado was permitted to resign his position as Governor of New Galicia, for as a ruler he had not proved particularly successful. As an explorer, however, he had covered a great amount of territory from the Grand Canyon on the west to Kansas and Indian Territory on the east, and north as far as the present state of Colorado. Concerning all this territory he brought back much interesting information.

Other Spanish explorers entered the territory, but it was not until the coming of Don Juan de Onate with 700 men and 130 families that a settlement was established. This settlement was made September 5th, 1598, at Chamita. Chamita was abandoned in 1605 and the settlement moved to Santa Fe. The Spaniards succeeded in conquering and enslaving the Pueblo Indians who occupied the country, and with their assistance they developed the mining, agricultural, grazing and other interests of the region for more than three-quarters of a century. In 1680, however, the Indians revolted. They burned ranch houses, destroyed other property and finally besieged the Spanish Governor in the old Governor's Palace at Santa Fe. On August 21st the Governor was forced to retreat and move southward. In October of the same year (1680) he reached El Paso with a company of 1,946 individuals, which included 300 friendly Indians. During this rebellion 401 persons, including 78 soldiers and 20 priests, were killed.

For the next twelve years (1680-1692) the Pueblos again controlled Santa Fe and they did their best to wipe out all traces of the Spanish domination. Spanish records were burned, Spanish mines were obliterated, the Spanish language was prohibited, and even the use of seeds introduced by the Spaniards was no longer permitted. This continued until 1692, when De Vargas was appointed Governor of the "lost province." With an army of 300 Spaniards and 100 Indians he overran the territory and in 1693 established himself in Santa Fe. Three years later there was another Indian outbreak, but this was soon put down by De Vargas. From the time of De Vargas until the year 1800 twenty-four Spanish governors ruled in the old Governor's Palace in Santa Fe.

Up until the beginning of the nineteenth century there had been no approach of Americans from the East into New Mexico. In 1804 an American peddler entered New Mexico, sold his wares at fabulous prices, and decided that he would remain in the country without bothering to render an account to his employer back east. The following year (1805) a hunter, trapper, and trader, named James Purseley became lost in the Rocky Mountains and wandered down into New Mexico. The following year Lieutenant Zebulon Montgomery Pike entered the San Luis Valley by mistake and built a fort.

He was arrested and taken to Santa Fe and later to Mexico.

In 1812 merchants from St. Louis blazed the now famous Santa Fe Trail, although this was not permanently opened until 1822. From this time trade rapidly increased and caravans of one sort or another were continually going and coming. By the year 1843 these caravans were very large, and single caravans which included 350 men and 230 wagons and carried nearly half a million dollars worth of goods at first cost were known.

In the year 1826 Kit Carson accompanied a party of hunters to Santa Fe and from that time until the time of his death in 1868, New Mexico was the center of many of his most interesting exploits.

From 1821 on, New Mexico was no longer under Spanish control. At that time she became a province of Mexico practically without bloodshed or disorder of any sort, and thus she remained until 1846 when General S. W. Kearney, marching westward from Fort Leavenworth, Kansas, occupied Santa Fe, and on August 22nd raised the American flag over the plaza and declared New Mexico a part of the United States. Not a shot was fired or a drop of blood spilled. By the terms of the Treaty of Guadalupe Hidalgo completed with Mexico February 2, 1848, at the close of the Mexican War this territory was ceded to the United States. A territorial government was soon set up, and in 1863 Arizona, which had originally formed a part of New Mexico, was set off as a separate Territory. In 1912 President Taft issued the formal declaration of statehood and New Mexico became a regularly recognized state of the United States of America. During the sixty years from 1851 to 1911 twenty-four different territorial governors served New Mexico.

The present state of New Mexico is almost square, extending approximately 350 miles east and west and the same distance north and south. Its area is 122,634 square miles, or 98 times the size of Rhode Island and larger than the United Kingdom of Great Britain and Ireland The altitude of the state varies from 13,360 feet to 2,876 feet, with an average altitude of more than one mile. There is an average of 214 clear days and 99 partly cloudy days each year. The resulting climate is mild, dry, and invigorating, although it varies greatly with the altitude. Many of the residents of the state have come as health-seekers attracted by the climate. The Rio Grande River flows for five hundred miles across the state from north to south.

In 1910 New Mexico ranked forty-fourth in population among the states. Her population in 1850 was 61,547; by 1860 it had increased to 93,516; in 1870 it was 91,874; in 1880, 119,565; in 1890, 160,282; in 1900, 195,310; in 1910, 327,301; and in 1914 the estimated population for the state was 383,551. In 1910 the density of population was 2.7 persons per square mile, as compared with 31 for the entire area of the United States. Of the total population in 1910, 280,730 were classed as rural and 46,571 as urban. Albuquerque was the only place in the state of 8,000 or over; its population was 10,020. The native white population was 281,940; the foreign-born white was 22,654. Of this latter group more than one-half came from Mexico, and of the native white group possibly sixty per cent were of Spanish and Mexican stock. There were 20,573 Indians in the state, and these were almost all Pueblo Indians. There were only 1,594 negroes in the state. So far as population is concerned the entire state was and is predominantly of Mexican or Spanish ancestry.

For many years the development of New Mexico was held back by lack of railroads. In 1878, however, the Atchison, Topeka and Santa Fe Railroad entered the state, and by February 15, 1880, it had been completed through to Santa Fe. There was considerable excitement over the building of part of this road, as the last 360 miles were built in 260 days in order to save the charter of the road. Soon after the road was completed through to El Paso. Later came the Denver and Rio Grande, the Southern Pacific and other roads. There are now nearly four thousand miles of main track in the state. Transportation facilities are, therefore, relatively good.

Another circumstance which delayed the development of New Mexico was the difficulty of getting a clear title to land. It was the custom of the early Spanish sovereigns to issue grants of territory to explorers and settlers. These grants often covered large areas. Later the land was parceled out on certain terms to loyal followers. When the Treaty of Guadalupe Hidalgo was made with Mexico in 1848 it contained a provision forever guaranteeing the validity of these original grants. Naturally this left matters in a very complex state and for a long time it was very difficult to get a clear title to any land which had been included in these early grants. For years Congress delayed action in this matter, but at last the Court of Private Claims was established and most of the questions of titles have now been settled and an individual can purchase land in New Mexico with as much legal security to the title as in other states.

So far as agriculture is concerned over eleven million

acres of land in New Mexico were laid out in farms in 1910, and the area has been steadily increasing since that time. An overwhelming proportion of this land is farmed by Spanish-speaking farmers. About one-third of these farms were irrigated farms. The climate of New Mexico differs so much in different parts and at different altitudes that in many places good crops can be raised without irrigation. The amount of irrigated land is, however, steadily increasing. On these farms millions of dollars worth of farm products are grown every year. These products include corn, wheat, oats, barley, potatoes, hay, beans, yams, apples, peaches, pears, plums, prunes, sugar cane, berries of many sorts, and other small fruits and vegetables. The mild climate and vast grassy plains of New Mexico make unusually favorable conditions for the raising of stock, and millions of sheep and cattle roam over her hills and valleys and supply yearly millions of pounds of wool and other animal products for our consumption. There is some lumbering in the state and a great deal of mining, particularly of coal and copper and of many other metals on a larger or smaller scale.

As a land of romantic and archæological interest, however, New Mexico stands perhaps unexcelled. Here Indian pueblos of traditional age and Mexican plazas of charming simplicity blend into the already beautiful landscape in a way to charm the eye of the artist. The thousands of little adobe houses scattered over hillside and valley, sometimes many miles from the beaten path of civilization, seem to form as integral a part of the everpleasing vista as do the bushes by the way, the projecting rocks, or the tumbling streams. Everything seems to "belong." One has only to visit New Mexico to feel that he is in an ancient land, a land of mystery, and a land with an untold past which must be full of interest. When the Spaniards arrived they found a very old civilization, how old no one knows. Some say the past of New Mexico goes back at least to 600 A. D. Very old indeed it is, and the very isolation of the life has tended to preserve its oldness. Some have called the state the "Holy Land" of America, for here as nowhere else in America can be seen the customs of the orient. Here the sickle is still in use; and here the ox and the goat may still be seen treading out the grain. Here the shepherd still lives with his sheep; and here the rugged mountain-side reminds the visitor of the rocky hills of Palestine. Here bricks are still made of straw; corn is ground between two stones; and beds are rolled up and taken along when on a journey. There is much in the life to suggest to the visitor that he has slipped back a few centuries into a life of which we have read, but which few of us have witnessed. The artist, the archæologist, the anthropologist, the ethnologist, the sociologist, and the student of folklore all find here in New Mexico a field which satisfies their longings, for there are ever new things to learn.

We do not have to go back into the prehistoric period, however, to find much that is of unusual interest. The old Governor's Palace in Santa Fe, of which we know the history, is perhaps as interesting and as full of romance as any of the prehistoric dwellings with which the state abounds. This Palace, built in 1605 of the ever-available adobe, still stands after more than three centuries of constant use. Here the long line of Spanish, Pueblo, Mexican, and American Territorial Governors has passed in continuous procession. This building, which antedates the settlement of Jamestown, New

Amsterdam, and Plymouth, has been through sieges and triumphs. It has housed executions and scenes of public thanksgiving. Here has floated the flag of Spain, the flag of Mexico, and the flag of the United States. Here murder has been committed, and here Lew Wallace as Governor of the Territory wrote the last part of Ben Hur, a tale of the Christ. Here in 1846 General Kearney formally took possession of New Mexico for the United States, and here he slept on the dirt floor after his long and weary march across the prairies. Or if one is not content he may walk across the ancient plaza and visit the famous old San Miguel Church, claimed to be the oldest church in the United States and to date back more than three hundred years. It is made of adobe and its walls are very thick. It is said that the bodies of many very important personages have been buried in this church, including the famous Spanish conqueror, De Vargas. Here can be seen and heard the famous bell, said to be the oldest bell in the United States, and just across the way stands the old adobe house which is claimed with equal enthusiasm to be the oldest dwelling in the United States. In Santa Fe one does indeed stand in the presence of the past, but a past which antedates the coming of the Spaniard nearly four hundred years ago by hundreds and possibly by thousands of years.

All this provides but the setting for the life of the present, but it is a setting which must be understood if the New Mexico of to-day is to be understood and if her problems are to be sympathetically and intelligently approached. New Mexico bears to-day the imprint of both the Spanish and the Mexican periods through which she has lived. The Spanish era left its language, its religion, its methods of agriculture, and many of its social customs indelibly stamped upon the region. The Mexican period, which was shorter and which occupied a time when Mexico herself was in turmoil and only just finding herself as a nation, possibly had a larger effect indirectly than directly upon the life of the region. Throughout all the Southwest there were many of Spanish and Mexican descent when the territory became a part of the United States three-quarters of a century ago. For the most part these settlers were of the independent, rugged, frontier type which had never been bothered with any undue enthusiasm for a central government of any sort. Their very isolation made their interests local. The fact, however, that the language of these people was Spanish as was the language of Mexico gave them a feeling of kinship with Mexico. Of course, too, the kinship was more than a mere feeling. On the other hand the stream of immigrants from Mexico has never ceased for more than three hundred years and the group which we adopted in 1848 has been steadily augmented both from within and from without. The fact that General Kearney was able to take over New Mexico without the shedding of blood, and the further fact that during the Civil War, which followed so soon after New Mexico had become a part of the United States, New Mexico stood loyal to the Union, are both indications that there never has been among our Spanish-speaking people of the Southwest any very pronounced pro-Mexico feeling. So far as they have been stirred by feelings of patriotism those feelings have been directed toward the United States. There has probably never been any real danger in the past that our Southwest would quickly turn against the United States in case of trouble with Mexico. The descendants of those who occupied this territory when we received it are of course

American citizens, "Spanish-Americans" we have come to call them. They are to be found throughout all of the Southwest, but they stand out most conspicuously in New Mexico. Both isolation and numbers have been factors in creating this situation.

At Santa Fe, both the ancient and the modern capital of New Mexico, there are to be seen some of the strangest sights which are to be witnessed in the United States. In politics the Spanish peaking element has always been and still is the dominant factor in the state. The Governor, a large number of the legislators, and a majority of all the other office holders in the state are of this group. When the legislature of the state meets, therefore, to transact business it becomes of the first importance that the speeches which are made and the remarks which are passed shall be interpreted so that all can understand. When a member speaks in English his remarks must be turned by the interpreter into Spanish so that those members of the legislature who do not understand English may know what he is talking about, and when another member speaks in Spanish the English-speaking members would be helpless without the aid of the faithful interpreter to interpret what has been said. Probably in no other state in the Union is the legislative business of the state conducted in two languages. And what is true of the legislative business is likewise true in court proceedings and in other activities of government where language is wont to be used.

Of course most of these Spanish-speaking officeholders are native-born American citizens. A few were born in Mexico. Most of them grew up in the United States and attended the public schools in New Mexico. The fact that they do not understand English is but an indication of the difficult task which the public school confronts in the teaching of English in communities where Spanish is the only language heard in the homes, on the streets, or on the playground. In the larger centers there is more incentive to master the English language, but in New Mexico there have been few "larger" centers. For the most part the people have lived tucked away in the mountains or hidden in the valleys sometimes fifty miles from the railroads, sometimes more. The roads are rough, often following the beds of mountain streams, so that during seasons of high water they are altogether cut off from the outside world and even during the more favorable seasons the difficulties of travel are so numerous that a trip"to town" is an event to be looked forward to for days and to be achieved only in the face of obstacles. One town in the central part of New Mexico visited by the writer during the spring of 1920 is more or less typical of scores of others.

It was situated fifty miles from the railroad, back in the mountains. All of the residents were Spanish-Americans with the exception of two mission school teachers. Spanish was the language spoken in every home in the community, and of the several hundred individuals in the town only two resident adults could speak English fluently. Most of the others could neither understand nor speak English. The nearest telephone was thirty-six miles away, the nearest doctor farther away than that, and groceries were hauled in over mountain roads for fifty-five miles, or only after 110 miles of travel for each load. To live permanently fifty-five miles from the nearest spool of thread, a trousers' button, or the simplest farm implement is to develop independence, initiative, and self-reliance, but it does not help greatly in the learning of a language which one in the very nature of the case can rarely or never hear spoken. In this particular town nearly everybody was related to nearly everybody else. The town has had an interesting history. More than fifty years ago a Mexican and his wife drove back into the wilderness and settled. There they raised a family. For the first few years they lived in a cave in the side of the mountain. Later they built an adobe house. As the children grew up they sought wives and husbands. A few people moved into the region and one after another little adobe houses and barns came into existence until the town has grown to its present size. As soon as spring appears the residents begin to scatter out to their little ranches distributed throughout the region. They raise their corn, and their beans, their oats, their wheat, their potatoes and various other crops. Their sheep, their goats, and their cattle forage on the mountainside or in the valley. In the fall the population once more returns to the town with the fruitage of the summer's labors.

In some of these higher altitudes in New Mexico the climate is surprisingly severe and sometimes the seasons are unfavorable. It is not to be wondered at that these people have only succeeded in securing the barest living. We should pause, however, before we jump to the conclusion that this indicates some native lack on the part of the people themselves. I have spent months at a time among the Highlanders of our Appalachian mountains and for industry, frugality, cleanliness, and general progressiveness these highlanders of the Southwest of Spanish and Mexican ancestry would seem to be on a par with those of the East who are of the best Scottish and Anglo-Saxon descent. Similar forces of environment have produced a similar result among peoples sometimes supposed to be very different. In each case we have a poor, but sturdy, independent, and self-reliant people. As a matter of fact the Mexican has never yet had a fair chance to show what he could make of himself. He has been held in subjection by autocratic political power and by a feudalistic social system which was bound to be dwarfing. Even in the early days of New Mexico a well developed feudalism prevailed. Sheep-growing was the great industry and we are told that at the beginning of the nineteenth century one single holding amounted to 2,000,000 sheep. The care of these required 2,700 persons always in the field, besides the thousands of others who were directly dependent upon them. These workers received little pay and it was very easy to get them into debt to the overlord, who thus held his workers in practical slavery.

For a time even after New Mexico became a territory of the United States practical peonage was authorized by law under an enactment entitled a "Law Regulating Contracts Between Master and Servant." This provided that a servant might leave his master's employ upon paying all that he owed to the master. This provision gave the master practically the continuous service of the servant. Since New Mexico became a part of the United States the chief obstacles to progress, however, have been ignorance, isolation, the barrenness of much of the country, and, for some time, the difficulty of getting a clear title to real estate. Gradually these untoward conditions are being removed, and there is every reason to believe that these Spanish-Americans will move out into more vital relationships to our national life as the years pass. The talk about the Mexican and the Spanish-American as "mañana" men is somewhat unfair, at least until we have had a chance to see what they can do with proper incentives and with adequate nourishment for their bodies. Up to date there is little to indicate that they have behaved particularly different from what other races would have behaved under similar circumstances. Nor should we assume that the Spanish-American is necessarily disloyal or unpatriotic merely because he does not speak the English language. The reason that he does not know English is that he has never been taught it, and in his limited sphere he has not felt particularly embarrassed by his ignorance. Of course we cannot permit him to remain permanently in this unfortunate condition, but it is a condition which cannot be altered overnight. Until it is altered the responsibility rests perhaps as much upon our shoulders as upon his. We have a large task, but there are few discouraging and many encouraging aspects of it. The present is a time for patience and a time for rendering every possible assistance to New Mexico within our power, as she grapples with a situation which is of national significance but the details of which must be worked out locally.

Governor O. A. Larrazola, the recent state executive, has been sharply criticized for his zeal for the teaching of Spanish in the lower grades of the public schools of the state. He is doubtless wrong in his judgment as to methods of procedure, but there appears to be nothing sinister in connection with his patriotic intentions and attitudes so far as the United States is concerned. He has zealously preached an orthodox Americanism, has taught respect for and urged allegiance to the American flag, and he has extolled the ideals of Christianity and the virtues of the Christian home.

For three-quarters of a century New Mexico has been a part of the United States. During that time she has made remarkable strides along every line. She got a late start, and physical conditions and differences of race have proved to be large, but not unsurmountable, difficulties. We are already proud of New Mexico and her Spanish-American population. They gave a good account of themselves both during the Civil War and during the late War, and they have given a good account of themselves in times of peace. Some day when educational facilities shall have been better developed and shall have had an opportunity to work their inevitable results we shall find it less natural to speak of them as "Spanish-Americans," for they will have lost their identity and have become merged in the great American populace which is made up of so many different strains and different mixtures and which we all fondly believe possesses the abilities and the virtues of them all.

CHAPTER IV

RELIGION

IF we are to understand the present religious situation among the Mexicans and the Spanish-Americans in the United States, we must recall a little of the historical background for it. The natives of Mexico were zealously religious even before the arrival of the Spaniards, and the religious authority was very closely identified with the political authority. This was particularly true under the Montezumas, the last of the Aztec rulers, and religious practices had become rather highly developed. Cortes and the other early Spanish explorers were accompanied by Catholic friars, and one of the avowed purposes of all the early explorations was the extension of the Christian faith among the heathen.

Thus when Panfilo de Narvaez petitioned in 1527 for a grant which was to include all of our southern gulf states, the northern part of Mexico, and New Mexico, he wrote: "Sacred Cæsarean Catholic Majesty: Inasmuch as I, Panfilo de Narvaez, have ever had and still have the intention of serving God and Your Majesty, I desire to go in person with my means to a certain country on the main of the Ocean Sea. I propose chiefly to traffic with the natives of the coast, and to take thither religious men and ecclesiastics approved by your Royal Council of the Indies, that they may make known and plant the Christian Faith. I shall observe fully what your Council require and ordain to the ends of serving God and Your Highness, and for the good of your subjects." This particular expedition met with many misfortunes, but the statement is typical of the time and of the entire period of Spanish domination.

The early Spanish expeditions to "New Spain" were all conceived with the avowed purpose of extending the ecclesiastical authority of the Catholic Church quite as much as to extend the political domination of Spain. The story of the spread of nominal Christianity became practically identical with that of Spanish conquest. The spread of missions in those days did not wait upon the slow processes of enlightenment, education, or persuasion. The rule of the Church was imposed as ruthlessly as the rule of the state. Thus De Vargas had no more than established himself in Santa Fe, after he had subdued the natives who had revolted some years before, than he sent back word to his Viceroy that he had "conquered for the human and Divine Majesties" all the pueblos for thirty-six leagues and had baptized nearly 1,000 children "born in rebellion." Thus in a sort of wholesale fashion Christianity was imposed upon the natives throughout New Spain. The story did not vary particularly in the different parts of the territory. During the entire period of Spanish domination and of Mexican independence the Church and the ecclesiastical authorities have been perhaps the dominating influence in determining the political fortunes of Mexico, for, in spite of the fact that the ecclesiastics stood, with few exceptions, strongly with Spain against Mexican independence, the power of the clergy was dominant in the new republic. One of the early acts of the new government was the passage (January 4, 1823) of a "National Colonization Law," of which the following paragraph is the first article:

"Article I. The government of the Mexican nation will protect the liberty, property, and civil rights of all foreigners who profess the Roman Catholic apostolic religion, the established religion of the empire."

Another article of the same law reads as follows:

"Article XVI. The government shall take care, in accord with the respective ecclesiastical authority, that these new towns are provided with a sufficient number of spiritual pastors, and, in like manner, it will propose to Congress a plan for their decent support."

It is needless to multiply illustrations of the close association of the ecclesiastical with the political authority, or to dwell upon the vast wealth collected by the Church. By 1850, however, it was estimated that the Church owned one-third of all the real and personal property of the Mexican Republic. The power of the Church became so vast and the conditions which it imposed became so intolerable, that an overturn of authority became next to inevitable. This came under Benito Pablo Juarez, an Indian by birth but one of the great leaders of Mexico. Under his influence the constitution of 1857 was made to provide for freedom of religious opinions, and two years later the complete separation of church and state and the confiscation of much of the Church property was brought about. The influence of the church in politics did not stop with the formal separation of church and state. The common people had become so dominantly Catholic that the influence of the Church upon all public affairs was still bound to be very large. Nor did the exploitations of the people by the Church cease.

As late as 1851 we are told by the author of "El Gringo" that in New Mexico the charge for spiritual services in connection with burials was so large that parents were known to abandon their children because they could not afford to pay for the burial charges of the church. He tells of one bill regularly made out and submitted of which he had personal knowledge which amounted to $1,600. This included a charge of approximately $1,000 for "los deréchos del obispo" (the rights of the bishop), and a charge of fifty dollars each for "los posos," which meant that each time the procession halted on the way to the burial a charge of fifty dollars was made. He tells of another bill of which he had knowledge which included charges for the following items: "Tolling of the bells," "the grave," "the grand cross," "high mass vestments," "holy water," "candlesticks," "vessel for incense," "resting places," "the interment," "mass," "use of the organ," "the chanters," "the response of the oratory," "the deacon's fee," and "additional." The charges for these items varied from one to thirty dollars each, and a bill made out in regular form was submitted by the ecclesiastical authorities and paid by the man who was so unfortunate as to lose any member of his family by death.

Up until 1850 in New Mexico and 1867 in Old Mexico the Catholic Church had no competition from Protestant churches. Protestant work has developed slowly. Within recent years, however, there has been a steadily growing feeling of dissatisfaction with the Catholic Church and its methods in Mexico, and in large areas the priests have, at times, literally been driven out of Mexico. While the revolution of 1920 which resulted in the overthrow of Carranza was in progress I talked with a prominent leader of the revolutionists concerning this religious question.

"What will be the attitude of the new government toward religion?" I inquired.

"It will be that of religious freedom and toleration," he replied; and then he continued, "For one I do not believe that we ought to drive out the Church. That won't work. The Mexican people are too religious for that, but I do believe that we must have religious liberty, and Protestant missionary work will be gladly welcomed by the new government, particularly the educational work."

The new government in Mexico evidently intends to give both the Catholic and the Protestant churches in Mexico every opportunity to carry on their regular activities, but the lessons of the past have not been forgotten, and there is a determination of steel to see to it that the blighting hand of Catholic ecclesiasticism shall never again dominate the government.

All of this may seem to have little to do with the religious situation among our own Spanish-speaking population, but as a matter of fact it has much to do with it; first, because New Mexico was so long a part of Old Mexico and, second, because out of this Mexican environment there have come hundreds of thousands of Mexicans into the United States recently, and, while they are mostly nominal Catholics, many of them are in a state of mental revolt against the only church with which they have been associated. This makes them particularly responsive to any sincere, sympathetic, and kindly, religious approach which is made to them. They are, therefore, more responsive to Protestant and other religious efforts than are the Spanish-American Catholics who have resided longer in the United States and who are not so familiar in recent years with the results of unrestrained Catholic domination which has so long blighted the life of Mexico and the Mexicans. Some of the charges against the Catholic Church in connection with its work among the Mexicans and Spanish-Americans in the United States do not form pleasant reading, but until they are faced frankly by ecclesiastical authorities and some solutions worked out there is little hope of these people taking their full place on an intellectual and moral level with the rest of our citizenry. The question is fully as much one of Americanization and of social morality as it is a religious question.

In the early days the natives were "converted" to Christianity at the rate of thousands per day practically at the point of the gun. It was inevitable that this acceptance of Christianity could be only a formal matter. The cross was substituted for or became an affix to some pagan ceremony. Even to-day in our Southwest the cross is an ever-present wayside decoration in scores of communities where vital Christianity is unknown. Heathen rites and Christian ceremonies became merged in something which was partly Christian in nomenclature and pagan in spirit and reality. Such wholesale extension of formal Christianity could result in nothing else. Christianity became a matter of form and ceremony, and Christianity as a way of life received little attention.

Religion and morality either became entirely divorced or religion became a convenient device for making immorality safe and innocuous. The "Bull of Composition" is said to have permitted the priests to relieve persons who stole property from the obligation of making restitution, provided that a certain sum, based on the value of the stolen goods, was paid to the priest. It was understood, however, that the ame person could not purchase more than fifty of such licenses in one year. As late as 1914 John Wesley Butler writes of Mexico, "Indulgences are still sold publicly." To-day we see the fruitage of such a system, for observers everywhere testify to the fact that Mexicans raised under such a sys em may have many virtues, but they will persistently steel and lie. Thus a Mexican who is a faithful worker and is a kindly, polite, and orderly citizen will lie amazingly and will take property which does not belong to him when opportunity offers. On the other hand, Mexicans raised under a different environment are as scrupulously truthful and honest as Americans.

Closely associated with this is the attitude of the Mexican toward marriage and the sex relationship in general. Here again the church by its exorbitant marriage fees has discouraged marriage and encouraged promiscuity. This, too, is unfortunate. The author of "El Gringo" tells us that after New Mexico became a part of the United States the very lowest marriage fee charged was $20, or the equivalent of a peon's wages for four months. From this amount the charges ranged up to at least $400. The list of abuses might be greatly extended. It should be borne in mind also that many Roman Catholic writers have spoken as freely of religious conditions in Mexico as have Protestant writers.

In 1865 Abbé Emanuel Domenech came to Mexico as chaplain of the French troops. Later he was asked by the Vatican to make a tour of the country and report upon "the moral and religious conditions of the clergy and Church." The following is quoted by John Wesley Butler from Abbé Domenech's report: "Mexican faith is a dead faith. The abuse of external ceremonies, the facility of reconciling God, the abuse of internal exercises of piety, have killed the faith in Mexico. . . . The idolatrous character of Mexican Catholicism is a fact well known to all travelers. . . . The mysteries of the Middle Ages are utterly outdone by the burlesque ceremonies of the Mexicans. . . . The Mexican is not a Catholic. He is simply a Christian because he has been baptized. I speak of the masses and not of the numerous exceptions to be found. . . . The clergy carry their love of the family to that of paternity. In my travels in the interior of Mexico, many pastors have refused me hospitality in order to prevent my seeing their nieces and cousins and their children." It should be remembered that these are the words of a Roman Catholic who has endeavored to understand the actual situation in Mexico.

It is not surprising that with such a background we find throughout the Southwest, but particularly in the secluded parts of New Mexico, religious beliefs, customs, and superstitions which have either never existed in other parts of the country or have been outgrown generations ago. Thus we read in the "Land of Poco Tiempo" by Charles F. Lummis that as late as 1887 a local witch was stoned to death in New Mexico for the crime of turning a perfectly respectable citizen into a woman for the space of three months. He also speaks of a number of people who have seen and held converse with "his Satanic Majesty." Possibly the most extreme manifestation of depraved religious practices at the present time is to be found among the Penitentes of New Mexico.

The origin of this peculiar Penitente order is somewhat in dispute. It has been easy to jump at the conclusion that they were connected in some historical manner with the "Flagellantes," an order which originated in the Middle Ages (Italy, 1210) and later spread throughout a large part of Europe. A more careful study seems to indicate, however, that the Penitentes of New Mexico (for they are to be found nowhere else except in the northeastern counties of New Mexico and to a slight extent in southern Colorado) are a continuation of the Third Order of Saint Francis. L. Bradford Prince, in his story of the "Spanish Mission Churches in New Mexico," says that this order introduced customs which could very easily be exaggerated and corrupted into the present Penitente customs and ceremonies. Benavides, the great Franciscan, in his report to the king in 1630, quotes an Indian wizard who was opposed to Christianity as saying: "You Spaniards and Christians are crazy and desire us to be so also. You are so crazy that you go along the streets lashing yourselves like madmen, shedding blood." To this Benavides adds, "He must have seen some disciplinary procession of Holy Week in some Christian pueblo."

There is every reason to believe that we have here the beginning of the Penitente customs. The Third Order of Saint Francis was composed of laymen and it was widely extended throughout New Mexico. Its purpose was to carry the principles of the life of Saint Francis into the life of the laity, and for two centuries nearly all of the leading citizens were members of the Order. This fact is borne out by the wills of the period which are said to have usually contained the following clause, "I direct that when God, our Lord, shall see fit to call me out of this present life, my body be enshrouded in the habit of our father, San Francisco, of whose Third Order I am a brother, and that my funeral be modest." This continued throughout the Spanish occupancy and until the Mexican Revolution, when the Franciscans were forced to leave the field and the supervision of the Third Order. The Penitentes, who seem to be the lineal descendants of this Third Order, came to call themselves "The Brotherhood of the Blood of Christ."

Some years ago this order was supposed to be dying out, but it has recently seemed to take on new life. This is said to be due quite largely to the encouragement of politicians who have discovered the political possibilities of the organization. I have not seen the articles of incorporation, but I am informed by a Spanish-American who has long been resident among the Penitentes of New Mexico that the order has recently been incorporated by the state of New Mexico under the name, "Sociedad de Nuestro Padre Jesus, De Nazareno" (The Society of Our Father Jesus, the Nazarene), and that many county and state officials in New Mexico owe their positions to the Penitentes. Mr. Lummis writes that in the year 1888 but "three towns in the Territory had Penitente processions and but one enjoyed a crucifixion." If Mr. Lummis was correct there has indeed been a considerable revival since that time, for in the year 1920 there are scores of towns where the Penitentes are the dominating political, social, and religious factor in the community. The Moradas or Penitente houses are usually made of stone or adobe, often without windows of any sort and marked only by a small wooden cross. Sometimes these buildings stand by the side of the Catholic church and sometimes at a distance from it. Sometimes they are out in the open and sometimes in out-of-the-way spots.

The meetings of the order are secret and it is not easy to know even who the members in a given community are. During Holy Week, however, some of their ceremonies and particularly their processions are in the open. The participants in these open processions wear a black mask over the entire head, so that even their neighbors do not know who is taking part. They wear a small lower garment, but aside from that and the mask their bodies are naked. Their backs are gashed with flint or some other sharp instrument, and then they whip themselves with whips m de of yucca or other harsh cactus, as they proceed on their weary march. Some carry wooden crosses of great weight to a distant hill; some wheel barrows of stone through impassable sand, and others draw heavy loads with cords which cut into their naked bodies. Many sorts of suffering are devised and these vary from community to community, inasmuch as there is little or no general supervision of the order. There is said to be a superstitious regard for the verse, "Without the shedding of blood there is no remission of sins." There is also on the part of some a desire to do sufficient penance at one time to last for the entire year. It should not be inferred, however, that these people are particularly contrite, for some of the worst characters appear to enter most zealously into the ritual and then to go out for another year of unimproved conduct. Actual crucifixions apparently no longer take place, but exposure and scourging often incapacitate the participants for longer or shorter periods. A reliable witness told the writer of a young man who was recently laid up for nearly six months, during a portion of which time he was at the point of death, as a result of participation in a Penitente procession. These Penitente processions have been witnessed by hundreds of people in spite of the fact that every possible secrecy is observed, and I have seen several relatively recent snapshots of participants in such processions.

For many years, particularly since the coming of Bishop Lamy in 1851, the Catholic Church has disapproved of the Penitente customs. In spite of that fact all of the Penitentes are supposed to be members in good standing of the Catholic Church and they usually succeed in holding a portion of their Holy Week exercises in the Catholic Church.

Of a similar superstitious nature is the reverence paid to the little old Catholic church at Chimayo, New Mexico. This object of pilgrimage and reverence is variously known as "Santuario, Chimayo" and as the "San Esquipula Church." It is a little adobe structure sixty by twenty-four feet in dimensions and with walls three feet thick. Picturesquely situated on the mountainside, miles from the railroad, in a most inaccessible region, it is the object of pilgrimage for Mexicans and Spanish-Americans from a wide area, including Arizona and parts of Old Mexico. The dirt enclosed in one room of this church is supposed to have miraculous properties, especially in the healing of sickness. As many as one hundred visitors have been known to visit the church in a single day, and on occasion pilgrims may be seen approaching the building on their hands and knees. Hundreds of people all over the Southwest attribute their present good health to the healing properties of the dirt in this famous church at Chimayo. A considerable hole has been dug in the dirt floor by pilgrims who insist on carrying home some of the earth. Old residents say that this earth was once used to allay the violence of storms and to ward off lightnings. The method used was to throw a few grains of the dirt into the fireplace; when the smoke reached the top of the chimney the fury of the storm abated and, if there were lightnings, they were turned aside. At present diseases are supposed to be healed by the drinking of a sort of tea made from the sacred earth or by the application of a portion of it to the diseased part of the body. This Church was privately built in 1816 by a prosperous Mexican. It is still under private control and has never been under the control of the priest. For many years, however, the priest ministered in it. The Church is said to be unique among all the churches of the Southwest in its reputation for the healing of disease.

It is needless to multiply illustrations of the way that ignorance, bigotry, and superstition have been woven into the very warp and woof of the religious life of the Mexicans and Spanish-Americans of our Southwest. If further illustration were needed we might note the legends concerning the miraculous painting of "Our Lady of Guadalupe" still perpetuated as truths, or the superstitious beliefs which have gathered about the famous De Vargas Day celebration in Santa Fé and other similar superstitious beliefs and practices. The fact is that the Spanish-Roman-Catholic domination of our Southwest has left our unfortunate Spanish-speaking citizens there with a heritage some of which dates back almost unchanged to the Middle Ages and which at its best is un-American and unfitted both in principle and practice to the needs of the Twentieth Century in which we live. For not the least of the errors which the Church has committed has been the refusal to raise up a native leadership, so that after 400 years we have the Church dominated by priests from France, Italy, Belgium, Spain and other European countries, priests who sometimes know little or nothing of the English language and who are ignorant of or out of sympathy with American ideals and institutions.

Unsatisfactory as has been the ministry of the Roman Catholic Church in this region, even this unsatisfactory ministry has failed to reach large numbers of the people, and the story has in many places been chiefly a story of neglect. The religious ministry in many communities consists of an infrequent visit from an itinerant priest. The poverty of the people has made the monetary returns small and the service has suffered as a result.

From a religious standpoint possibly nothing would be better for our Spanish-speaking Americans than for the Roman Catholic Church to frankly acknowledge her shortcomings in the past and to embark upon an educational campaign designed to substitute a religion of enlightenment for a religion of superstition; a religion of righteousness for one of formality; a religion of service for one of moral and financial exploitation; a religion of Americanism for a religion of un-Americanism; and a native trained leadership for a European trained leadership. The Roman Catholic Church holds the key to unlock the new day in our Southwest, so far at least as our Mexicans and Spanish-Americans are concerned, if she will but use it. If she refuses some one else must do the job.

It should not be inferred, of course, that the Protestant church is to have no place in ushering in the new day. She already has a large part in the task, and although she has sometimes moved haltingly she has made a far larger contribution to the religious and moral life of the people among whom she has been working than any results in terms of membership constituency might seem to indicate. She began her work about 1850 and she was, therefore, some 325 years behind the Roman Catholic Church in the same field. In the early days there was much persecution of Protestant workers; they were threatened, stoned, and, in at least one or two cases, killed. At present Protestant work for Mexicans and Spanish-Americans is being carried on in some 300 different communities in our border states. There is a reported membership of more than 10,000 and a Protestant constituency of several times that number. In the early days the work consisted largely of preaching and Sunday-school activities. Very soon an educational work was developed and more recently an elaborate social program has been undertaken. This is particularly true since the large influx of Mexicans into the United States has brought congestion and multiplied social problems into many communities in the Southwest. This social service program takes on many forms. It includes the maintaining of employment agencies; the furnishing of work and the teaching of trades through "Goodwill Industries"; the establishment of medical and dental clinics; home visitation; the teaching of English; the teaching of Spanish; instruction in music, elocution, practical nursing, health, hygiene, sanitation, manual training of many sorts, and other branches. Mothers are taught sewing, cooking, home-making, and the care of children in Mother's Clubs; and Boy Scout, Girl Scout, and many other clubs are maintained for boys and girls and young people. Mexicans in trouble and sickness are assisted; milk is distributed to undernourished children and to invalids; reading and rest rooms and information bureaus are maintained; and kindergartens are conducted. Day schools are conducted among Spanish-Americans and in Border towns, and Protestant boarding-schools for Spanish-speaking youth are to be found in all the Border states. In many places playground apparatus is provided, and community activities promoted. These include community celebrations, war-time garden projects, "clean-up" weeks, and other similar projects.

Much of this work is done purely as a service to the individual and the community, and no strings are attached to it. It is pure Americanization work done in the spirit of Christian service. Whenever possible a small charge is made for services rendered, in order that the habit of dependence and pauperization may not be encouraged. There is nothing of exploitation and little or nothing of "proselytism" in connection with this fine and rapidly extending social ministry. Its primary purpose is to assist an unfortunate and often helpless people to establish themselves upon an American plane of living. As a by-product this work is doing much to establish confidence on the part of Mexicans in Americans and in America, and new arrivals in America have proved to be remarkably open to approach and remarkably grateful when they have once become convinced that certain Americans, at least, stand ready to help them during the difficult period of getting established in a new land, merely because they are fellow human beings in need.

In this fine work many independent agencies are assisting. Thus the Y. M. C. A. has several Mexican branches where Mexican boys and young men are receiving under a wholesome environment the same sort of opportunities and training as is accorded to American youth. The Y. W. C. A. used a portion of its war fund for Americanization work among Spanish-speaking people on the Border. A number of centers were opened from San Antonio through to Los Angeles. As the original funds have become exhausted, the work has in some cases been adopted locally. In these centers a great variety of activities has been carried on. Hundreds of Mexican girls and women have been gathered in English classes, cooking classes, and home-making clubs of many sorts. The teaching of history and American civics has been included, and the work has reached not only the poorer Mexican women but also some of the wealthiest and most aristocratic among the refugees. In Pirtleville, Arizona, the work has included a fine ministry to the boys and girls of the community, the establishment of a community reading room, the distribution of quantities of magazines and other periodicals, and various other ministries. In El Paso a room has been set aside for the use of Mexican girls employed as shop girls and as stenographers, to which they can come during the noon hour to prepare and eat their mid-day lunch. Thus the list of ministries carried on by these and other agencies might be greatly extended. They are but illustrations of the way in which America is extending the hand of friendship to our newly arrived neighbors from Old Mexico. They represent one of the most hopeful aspects of the entire Border situation.

It is needless to talk about the "rights" of the Protestant church to work in this field. In a land of religious freedom there will always be opportunity for earnest Christians to proclaim the truth as they see it. In this field, however, there has been the challenge of great need to which the Protestant church could do no less than respond. There will, without doubt, always be a Protestant constituency here, and very likely it will be a steadily increasing constituency. The responsive attitude of the newcomers from Mexico seems to promise this, particularly when the present enlarged program of Christian work on the part of the Protestant agencies is taken into consideration. On the other hand, a Protestant membership constituency of something over ten thousand souls as the result of three-quarters of a century of effort does not promise any quick solution of the religious problem in this field by the conversion of our Spanish-speaking population to the Protestant faith. If the solution of the matter depended upon this, the situation would indeed be discouraging. Quite apart from numbers the Protestant Church has brought into the field higher ideals of life and conduct, a more wholesome interpretation of God and of Jesus Christ, and an attitude of unadulterated Americanism which has had a wide influence upon the life of the Southwest, including the Roman Catholic Church.

There have been many fine, self-sacrificing, and devoted Catholic leaders in the Southwest, but they have been handicapped by a heritage so corrupt and a system so un-American that their best efforts have been largely nullified. And yet the future of our Spanish-Americans would seem to lie in the hands of the Catholic Church unless that institution persists in "sinning away its day of grace." If she will but substitute a religion of truth for one of superstitution: if she will put as much emphasis upon conduct and social morality as she now puts upon ceremony; if she will substitute Americanism for un-Americanism; if she will raise up and substitute a native leadership for a foreign leadership; if she will substitute service for exploitation; and if she will assist every Spanish-speaking member of her constituency in the United States to master and speak the English language, she will render a service for which we shall as a nation have genuine cause for thanksgiving and which will help us to forget some of the errors of the past.

CHAPTER V

EDUCATION

THE many recently arrived Mexican families in the United States have placed the school systems of our Southwestern states under an unusual strain. The mere increase in numbers, coming as it did at a time when attention and energy were taken up with the World War, was sufficient embarrassment in countless communities, but the introduction of a large group of non-English-speaking children brought with it complications and problems which have proved much more difficult of solution than has the mere problem of numbers. These considerations, added to the fact that both New Mexico and Texas have been slow in bringing their public school systems to efficiency, and to the further fact that schools all over the United States have recently been seriously embarrassed by a shortage of teachers and other post-war conditions, have accentuated an already difficult situation.

Writing in "El Gringo" as early as 1857, W. W. H. Davis said: "The standard of education in New Mexico is at a very low ebb, and there is a larger number of persons who cannot read and write than in any other Territory in the Union. The number attending school is given as 460, which is about one scholar to every 125 inhabitants. . . . This exhibits a fearful amount of ignorance among the people, and it is enough to make us question the propriety of intrusting them with the power to make their own laws. It was always the policy of Spain and Mexico to keep her people in ignorance, and, so far as New Mexico was concerned, they seem to have carried out the system with singular faithfulness, and in no country in the world that lays tne least claim to civilization has general education and a cultivation of the arts been so generally neglected. . . . There is not a native physician in the country, nor am I aware that there has ever been one."

At best, 460 pupils in a population of 61,547 does not make a very satisfactory showing. Matters did not improve rapidly, however, when New Mexico became a Territory of the United States. The Federal government did little at first to promote education and New Mexico did not have a public school law until 1891.

It should be said, however, that the New Mexico Territorial Legislature passed a bill at its 1855-1856 session establishing a common school system to be supported by public taxation. The measure was submitted to the people, and thirty-seven votes were cast for it; a total of 5,016 votes was recorded as opposed to the measure. It is worthy of mention that about this time the United States government sent a box of books as a gift to the Territory with which it might start a territorial library. The territorial legislature, however, refused to pay the freight charges on the books and left them to be sold for the freight or destroyed by the freight agent. Dr. Thomas Harwood, who spent half a century in New Mexico, says that in 1870 "not a public school house could be found, hardly a Bible in one family in a thousand, and only a few other books; hardly a public road or a bridge; . . . hardly an American plow, wagon, or buggy."

In 1910, 48,697 persons of ten years of age or over, or 20.2 per cent of the total population of the state, were reported as illiterate.

The latest biennial report of the State Superintendent of Public Instruction, published in 1918, gives the total school population (5 to 21 years) of New Mexico as 121,829, of whom 86,699 were enrolled in school. The average attendance was 56,398. For the state 1,413 schoolhouses were reported, and a total of 2,641 teachers was employed. A recent investigation by the Russell Sage Foundation into the efficiency of the different school systems in the United States places New Mexico thirty-first among the states of the Union. This rating is said to have been based upon a study of attendance, training given, progress made by pupils, amounts expended for buildings and supplies, salaries paid, and other similar items. New Mexico seems, therefore, to have made very encouraging progress in connection with her schools. Such a report cannot, however, in the very nature of the case, tell the whole story, for New Mexico is unique among the states.

The language question is ever' at the front in New Mexico. Shall it be English, or shall it be Spanish? The Governor and a certain group of officials have had one idea and another group has had another idea. Governor Larrazola is reported to be strongly in favor of having the first few years of instruction given in Spanish in communities where it is desired. This plan has not yet been legalized in the state, however. The present state law provides, "That Spanish as a separate subject shall be taught in any public elementary or high school in the state when a majority vote of the board of school directors or board of education in charge of such school shall direct" . . . but that, "Except as herein provided, the books used and the instruction given in said schools shall be in the English language; provided that Spanish may be used in explaining the meaning of English words to Spanish-speaking pupils who do not understand English."

The law is perhaps beyond reproach, but it is only fair to say that, in the rural regions particularly, it does not operate to produce any very great facility in the use of the English language among pupils who come to school from Spanish-speaking homes. The reason of course is not far to seek. Thousands of pupils come to the public school who have never spoken a word of English. Very likely their teachers are also from Spanish-speaking homes. It is inevitable that under those conditions much of the conversation in the schoolroom will be in Spanish, while on the playground and at home Spanish is the only language heard or used. The ability to pronounce a few English words from a book, words the meaning of which is often unknown, does not add greatly to the pupil's knowledge of a language which is strange to him and which he has little occasion to use in school and no occasion to use outside of school. Thus I rode recently for two days over the mountains of New Mexico with a Spanish-American, a citizen, born and raised in the United States and trained in the public schools of New Mexico, and yet, if his life had depended upon his ability to have spoken a complete sentence in the English language, I do not think that he could have accomplished the feat. And his case is more or less typical of the cases of thousands of others, who under similar conditions grow up without being able to read either English or Spanish and with a speaking knowledge of Spanish only. We face here a very difficult situation and one which calls neither for harsh criticism nor for harsh measures, but rather for sympathy, helpfulness and insight. There are many factors involved here in addition to the simple pedagogical matter of teaching a language. Of course the language must be taught persistently and insistently, but what is one going to do with it after he has learned it if it is a language which his father and mother and his neighbors do not understand. It would seem that these communities which are so distinctly Spanish to-day must inevitably pass through a bi-lingual period before English can finally dominate, and during that period the school has an unusually important and an unusually difficult task to perform. In communities where there is a larger proportion of Anglo-Saxon stock the problem is a simpler one, unless, as happens in many cases, the Spanish element becomes segregated and lives largely to itself. The whole problem is aggravated by the tendency of Spanish-American boys and girls to cut the school years as short as the law will alloy, and in many cases even shorter than that.

In the larger centers along the Border, such as San Antonio, El Paso, Los Angeles, and others, we have similar problems with all sorts of variations.

As early as 1915 Miss Elizabeth Barbour, School Superintendent for Brownsville, Texas, said, in speaking of her pupils in Brownsville, "of those entering the first grade, ninety-two per cent are unable to understand one word of English, much less to speak it. Those of you who have three or four such children in your classes can have no idea of what it means to have the numbers reversed and have three or four English-speaking children among a class of non-English-speaking ones." Some of these children of whom Miss Barbour speaks were not only American-born but of American-born parents, and some of American-born grandparents. All of these Border towns have recently received a fresh influx of Mexicans. From these Mexican homes come throngs of bright boys and girls with all the good wishes of fond parents who want their children to enjoy all of the advantages which American children have. In an overwhelming proportion of cases, however, their hopes are doomed to disappointment. The entire trail of the public school in the Southwest is strewn with the blasted hopes of Mexican boys and girls. By the time high school is reached there are few left, and of those who complete a high school course the number is small indeed. The proportion varies from city to city, but in general it is always small and sometimes almost negligible. In San Antonio, for example, where 11,000 Mexican pupils are enrolled in the city schools, only 250 were found in high school and not more than ten Mexican graduates were included in a recent graduating class. In El Paso with one half of the grade pupils of Mexican parentage the ratio in the high school is 100 in a total enrollment of 1,400. Recent graduating classes have had from four to ten Mexican students. The Superintendent, A. H. Higby, says "The Mexican children drop out in great numbers at about the fourth grade," Mr. Harry M. Shafer of the Los Angeles city schools says, "Very few Mexican pupils reach the high school and almost none graduate from high schools." Public school authorities have been frank to place part of the blame for this situation upon a course of study conceived for use with American boys and girls and upon methods designed for use with pupils who come from a different environment and who already understand the English language. There is no doubt that part of the difficulty lies here, but there are many

other contributing causes such as economic pressure, undernourishment which undermines ambition, the absolute
lack of home assistance, and, perhaps not least, a native
sensitiveness which makes unfavorable comparison with
other pupils unendurable. This latter factor is accentuated in communities where bitter race prejudice has been
allowed to develop, in some cases making the life of a
Mexican pupil well-nigh intolerable so long as he stays in
school. Fortunately, this condition is not universal, but
it is becoming altogether too common especially in Texas
towns.

Speaking of the Mexicans in San Antonio, W. J. Know
says:

"They will deny themselves the bare necessities of life
that their children may be supplied school books. Nothing
that will benefit or uplift is withheld. Not only do they
think of their own, but you will find in nearly every family
some orphan who receives the same consideration as their
own child. As is often the case with foreigners, you
never hear of a Mexican taking his child out of school for
the reason that it has had opportunity enough and must
go to work to repay parents. The children are only taken
out of school for sheer need, or because they are over-
sized and ashamed to be with smaller ones, or because
of race prejudice against them being so strong that they
forego an education rather than submit to the conditions
imposed."

Unfortunately one or more of these factors is at work
in a sufficient number of cases to make the life of the
Mexican pupil in many cases a very unpleasant one, and
to make him welcome an interruption of his school activities. Of those who do persist in school a large proportion are from the better Mexican homes where better

opportunities and more adequate food are available. It should be noted, however, that the child of a Mexican peon does not differ in mental ability from the more fortunate Mexican child, as a peon is only a poor Mexican. The language difficulty is of course a serious one. The Mexican pupil is not only expected to learn all that an English-speaking pupil learns but to learn it in a language which he does not understand. Much of the time he does not know what his teacher is talking about, and the tendency is to learn the English which he does learn in a parrot-like fashion. Even in the schools which are made up largely or exclusively of Mexicans or Mex-Americans the pressure to "make the grade" each year is often the same as in other schools, so that at best the pupil faces a very difficult task. Some schools provide separate classes for those who do not understand English. In California some cities segregate the children of Mexican parentage during the first three years of school life. In congested Mexican centers segregation becomes almost automatic, and in some cases, particularly in Texas, race prejudice brings about segregation.

Of course the child of poorer Mexican parentage is always handicapped both in ideals, incentives, and actual achievement by the limitations of his home environment. The ignorance of the Mexican is always the bond which binds both him and his children. This ignorance often extends to the simplest details which teachers may perhaps be excused for taking for granted. Thus a social worker recently found a girl in a poor Mexican home in distress. She had been told to write a composition upon the "cow in commerce," but a sympathetic conversation with her revealed the fact that she did not know that beefsteak came from a cow or that butter was made from milk. The utter lack of home guidance had left her to grow up at the mercy of her pitifully limited environment. Nor is the problem of attendance an easy one to solve among Mexicans in the United States. There is much seasonal work and much moving from place to place, and there are many other factors present to complicate the situation. In the city the task is always difficult, and in the country it becomes in some cases almost hopeless. For example, the report of the Commissioner of Elementary Schools for the State of California published in 1919 states casually that a recent visit to Imperial County has revealed the fact that there are hundreds of pupils of school age not in school, and this in spite of the diligent efforts of attendance officers. Now Imperial County is one of the very southern counties of California on the Mexican Border and inhabited by thousands of Mexicans. The same condition of non-attendance at the public schools can be duplicated in practically every rural region in the Southwest inhabited largely by Mexicans. In Texas it is only recently that there has been a compulsory education law. For the year beginning September 1, 1916, a total of sixty days' attendance was required of children between eight and fourteen years of age; in 1917 this was raised to eighty days; and in 1918 to 100 days. There are, however, numerous exceptions, as, for example: "Any child living more than two and one-half miles by direct and traveled road from the nearest public school supported for children of the same race and color of such child, and with no free transportation provided." In the same way, "Any child more than twelve years of age who has satisfactorily completed the work of the fourth grade of a standard elementary school of seven grades, and whose services are needed in support of a parent or other person standing in parental relation to the child" may be exempted from further attendance at school. In New Mexico the period of compulsory school attendance is from six to sixteen years, except that pupils fourteen years of age or over may be excused from school if they are gainfully employed.

In spite of limitations, however, the public school is probably rendering a larger service and accomplishing more in the way of Americanization in our Border states than any other institution. For it is a work of Americanization, no matter whether the particular pupil concerned is the child of a Mexican refugee, only temporarily in the United States, or whether he is destined to become a full-fledged American citizen and spend his life in this country. During the World War a large amount of patriotic training was introduced into the public schools, and it was not at all uncommmon to see the children of recently arrived Mexican parents shouting as vigorously for the United States and waving the American flag as energetically as native-born American children.

The field of education has not been left entirely to the public school, however. The Roman Catholic Church organized some parochial schools at an early date, and there are still a number of such schools serving Spanish-Americans, particularly in New Mexico. A work which has been of larger significance from the standpoint of general training and the promotion of Americanism has been done by the Protestant churches. As early as 1852 Protestant mission school work for Mexicans was begun at Brownsville, Texas, and about the same time schools began to be opened in New Mexico. For a long time education in New Mexico was largely confined to church schools. A great many of these schools have been conducted, and their influence has been incalculable. The custom has been for Protestant agencies to give up their distinctive day schools as soon as communities have been in a position to give satisfactory elementry education to their boys and girls, and in some cases even long before that ideal state has been attained.

During the year 1919-1920 forty Protestant mission schools were in existence in the four Border states of Texas, New Mexico (including a small part of Southern Colorado), Arizona, and California. Eighteen of these schools are boarding-schools, as follows: Eight girls' boarding-schools, seven boys' boarding-schools, and three co-educational schools. There are two girls' boarding-schools in California and one for boys; in Arizona there is one girls' boarding-school and none for boys; there are six boarding-schools in New Mexico, two for girls, two for boys, and two co-educational; Texas has eight of these Protestant boarding-schools, three for girls, four for boys, and one co-educational. The chief centers of this boarding-school work are Santa Fé and Albuquerque, New Mexico; El Paso, San Antonio, and Laredo, Texas; Tucson, Arizona; and Los Angeles, California. The Protestant day schools which remain are to be found chiefly in New Mexico and Texas.

These mission schools for Mexicans in the Border states represent a property investment of something over a million dollars, a teaching staff of 157, and an annual budget of not less than $150,000. Just at present this figure bids fair to be largely increased by the erection of new building and the addition of needed equipment. One school alone is putting $100,000 into additional buildings. During the year 1919-1920 3,210 pupils were enrolled in these

Protestant mission schools for Mexicans and Spanish-Americans.

Something of the popularity of these schools may be gathered from the fact that although tuition is charged at practically all of these schools they are in most cases filled to overflowing. During the year 1919-1920 one school alone turned away more than 150 applicants for admission and for whom it had no room. In New Mexico it is particularly striking that hundreds of Spanish-American parents pay their taxes to support the public school and then voluntarily pay tuition to send their children to a Protestant mission school in the same community. And this is done in spite of the fact that the parents are for the most part Catholics and in spite of the strong and often bitter opposition of the itinerant priest. The fact that the standard of instruction is higher in the mission school than in the public school and that in many cases the mission school offers the one opportunity to learn the English language accounts for its popularity. Then, too, the fine unselfish spirit of the mission school teachers has won the confidence of the people. No undue religious pressure is put upon the pupils in these schools, but there is a persistent attempt to inculcate the Christian virtues and to hold up Christian ideals of life and conduct before the pupils. The only pupils who consistently and persistently refuse to attend these schools in the communities where they exist are the children of Penitentes. On the Border these schools often serve an important international constituency, and scores of Mexican boys and girls come regularly across the international line to attend Protestant mission schools.

Nor are these pupils of mission schools all from the poorer homes. Many of them come from homes of

Mexican government officials of importance. General Emilio Salinas, brother-in-law to Carranza, and formerly Mexican Consul in New York City, sent his son to a missionary boarding-school conducted by the Methodist Episcopal Church, South, at Laredo, Texas. Another Mexican consul has several children at present attending another mission school in California, and the list might be greatly extended of similar cases on either side of the Border. The young woman who was stenographer to former President Madero of Mexico recently graduated from a mission school in California, and expects to give her life in service to her people. A young man, who, at the time the United States Army entered Vera Cruz, was an officer under Villa, came across the Border, was reached by a home missionary and is now studying in a mission school to prepare himself for the Christian ministry.

The training in these mission boarding-schools includes elementary, secondary, and many special courses. One school is planning to extend its course to include a full college training. At present the girls are taught cooking, sewing, music, and various household arts in addition to the regular elementary and secondary courses offered. At Holding Institute, Laredo, Texas, one of the most popular departments, both among the girls and the boys, is the business department, where stenography, typewriting bookkeeping and other related branches are taught. Several schools are located on large farms; the Texas-Mexican Institute at Kingsville, Texas, has 700 acres and the boys spend half a day in the schoolroom and half a day at work on the farm; the Rio Grande Institute at Albuquerque, also on a large well-equipped farm, furnishes similar opportunities for various kinds of farm training.

Many schools have wood-working or other manual training. At the Spanish-American Institute for boys at Gardena, California, one of the popular departments is the printing department. This fine, well-equipped department not only trains skilled printers but it incidentally does all of the school printing and handles a large volume of outside work. As one of its activities it publishes every two weeks a paper entitled "The Mexican Boy." The writing, editing, typesetting, and printing of this paper are done by the boys themselves as a part of their training. The Lydia Patterson Institute in El Paso is planning to add to its present excellent course a printing department, tailor shop, carpenter shop, shoe shop, and an auto shop. These are only illustrations of the varied training which these mission schools are rendering and are projecting for the future.

The boarding-school seems to offer an unusually good opportunity for non-English-speaking pupils to get that personal contact with their teachers which seems to be almost indispensable to satisfactory progress. Graduates and former pupils of these schools are everywhere giving a good account of themselves; some have gone on to college and then to professional schools of different sorts; and they have filled every sort of position from that of state legislator to sheep herder. Some are ministers, some are Y. M. C. A. secretaries, some are in business, many are teachers, and many have gone out to establish Christian, American homes after years of living in the environment of a Christian boarding-school. In some sections of New Mexico a large proportion of the public school teachers have been trained entirely or in part in mission schools. Thus in many ways the mission schools for Mexicans in the Southwest are exerting an Americanizing and a Christianizing influence quite out of proportion to the actual numbers enrolled in the schools. The following is the first composition in English written by a little Mexican girl in a mission school, after she had mastered the language enough to begin to write in it:

A MEXICAN GIRL'S COMPOSITION

"One apon time live a boy, has (his) name were Frank. He Askt has mother for nice party on Holloheen night. Mother sed all right if you be good boy. It was Holloheen night in the little house and it looked so perty with somany flags and punkens and paper turkeys.

"The Yacalentars (Jack-o-Lanterns) were all lighted bright and many friends come to Frank's house and his mother made a many pis and cakes. When friends come they smelled chile cooking and said, 'What a perty smell.'

"In the center of little house they had picnic with a table of punkens and cranberres and somany kinds of fruit and pi. Frank received a big package and he got so happy and then he say 'Everbodie get round me' and then everbodie looked in package. Everbodie beginning to laughed. There was a big bone and a dead rat.

"Frank say 'Everbodie danse.' He gets his girl to piano. Mother pulled his ears and hit him so hart and made a ball (bump) on his head an everbodie got scare. Mother say 'I tole you I don wan see you dansing.' Party stop and all say good nite."

In contrast to the foregoing and illustrative of the progress both in the use of English and in the inculcation of lofty ideals and patriotic sentiments which takes place in the mission schools is the following essay written by a Spanish-American boy about to graduate from the high school department of the Menaul School in Albuquerque:

PATRIOTISM

"Patriotism is love of country. It is that sentiment which enables us to study, deeply interested, our country's past, with intentions of learning what it stands for. It is this sentiment which makes great statesmen out of mere men, men who sacrifice everything for their country. It leads us to watch the progress of our country, do all in our power to insure and nothing to prevent it. A real patriot watches the program of his country and sees himself an actor taking an important rôle in it. He is a man who looks to his duty before his rights.

"To what do we attribute the success with which our army was organized during the world war? Why is it that labor and capital both forgot their troubles? Was it not a crime punishable by imprisonment to spread propaganda of any sort against our government? What was it that brought our soldiers to regard each other as brothers regardless of nationality? We were big enough then to overlook petty questions. All was done to secure our success as a nation. 'Unity, team-work,' we said, 'will bring about the victory of our armies.' We had rights as we have now, but duty came first; rights were ignored.

"Certainly America has been the melting pot of the world. But in this pot, no one will doubt, there is a residue which needs a higher temperature to melt it. Not so much legislation as warm American hearts. We have been cold to the foreigner. We must be interested in him if we are to make him a true American citizen. These people have acquired very different habits of living, consequently it is hard for them to break away suddenly from these habits. It is only by realizing that they are really our brothers that they can come to learn our language and, in turn, our customs.

"This war did away, in a great measure, with both class

and race distinction, but it also made the foreigner proud. He learned that he could do work equal to any man's, that he could fight as well as others. No wonder that we do not find him as submissive as before. The hyphenated American is to blame for not making himself thoroughly American, as is the so-called American for not giving him a better chance. Neither is willing to make any sacrifice for the good of the country. It was an extreme sense of patriotism which made us love our brothers. It was all to insure our country against any possibility of its working power being reduced. But where is this love of country gone? Why not give as much of our energy to insure the progress of our country now as we did during the war? Why not be as great a civilian nation as we were a soldier nation?

"We have a patriotism that is extremely beneficial to a country and another that ought never to exist. There are people who leave their mother country for one reason or another. They see some advantage in the country to which they go. But when they get there they do not swear allegiance from their hearts to that country which offers them better opportunities. This kind of ore coming into our melting pot is absolutely out of place in our country. We say nothing against this patriotism, but if we must love our mother country wherever we are the best thing to do is to stay there and cause no trouble elsewhere by a too deeply rooted patriotism. If Greek, Italian, French or Mexican comes here and remains so our pot has no power over them. We shall have to cast them away as worthless slag.

"It has been proven that patriotism makes us act as a body, brings us to see our relations to each other. Then why not bring this sentiment back into our hearts and keep it forever there? It is the keynote to national and individual prosperity."

The foregoing may have some defects as an essay, but as an expression of pure Americanism and as an illustration of the contribution which mission schools are making to the lives of thousands of our Spanish-speaking boys and girls in the Southwest it is pertinent.

The educational task among Mexicans and Spanish-Americans in the United States is not, however, limited to the period of childhood and youth. We face the problem of dealing with hundreds of thousands of adults who do not speak the English language and who do not understand our customs and our forms of government. A recent study of 1,081 Mexican families in the Plaza section of Los Angeles revealed the fact that fifty-five per cent of the men and seventy-four per cent of the women could not speak English; sixty-seven per cent of the men and eighty-four per cent of the women could not read English; and seventy-five per cent of the men and eighty-five per cent of the women could not write English. Of the families studied, more than sixty per cent had been in Los Angeles more than three years; fifteen per cent had been in the City less than a year. The excellent work done by the public schools and other agencies of Los Angeles makes it seem likely that the situation here, so far as illiteracy is concerned, is better than in many other centers.

Up to date no very great progress has been made in the teaching of English to adults of Mexican origin. A number of churches have maintained, and are maintaining, English classes for adults. The Goodwill Industries of Southern California teaches English to its employees. The Y. W. C. A., at its International Institutes, has enrolled some hundreds of adults in English classes, and the pupils have included representatives from some of the more prosperous Spanish-speaking homes in the United States. Various other social agencies have done more or less of this work. The total of all adults included in English classes has, relatively speaking, been small. Most adults have been left to pick up the English language in connection with their regular employment, and, when this does not provide the opportunity to learn English, the opportunity has not been provided. In the case of the women the opportunity has very naturally been much less than in the case of the men, and this has been unfortunate for a number of reasons. For example, in cities where unprecedentedly high wages are being offered for housework Mexican women are unable to qualify for the positions offered because they are not familiar with American ways of housekeeping and because their language limitations will not permit them to ask questions or to receive instructions from their would-be employers.

The language question is such a large and important one that it is to be doubted whether adequate progress will be made in handling it until it is taken up systematically by some state or national agency. On the other hand, there is a real embarrassment on the part of certain Mexican young people in the United States, because of the limited facilities offered for perfecting themselves in the use of Spanish and for training in Spanish literature. A considerable number of these Americanized young folks later become teachers of public schools in Mexico, and they must, in order to do this, perfect themselves in Spanish. Some schools on the Border, therefore, make much of the study of Spanish, and in some cases, particularly where a school is serving regularly an international constituency, all instruction is given both in English and in Spanish. Of course it may be argued that we are not obligated to train teachers for schools in Old Mexico. On the other hand, it is to be doubted whether we could do any finer piece of service for Mexico than to do just that thing. A generation of teachers trained in American schools and inculcated with American ideals would not only do much for Mexico, but it would provide a surer and cheaper protection for the United States than armies and navies can ever furnish.

In many informal ways educational work is extended among Mexicans in the United States. Through mothers' clubs many sorts of instruction are given, such as instruction in the care of babies, the preparation of food, the care of the home and similar subjects. For the young people there is a limited number of literary clubs, debating societies, branch libraries, Boy Scouts, Girl Scouts, Boy Indians, sewing classes, business classes, wood-working classes, basket ball teams, kindergartens, day nurseries, baseball clubs and numerous similar organizations and activities carried on in connection with various churches, social centers, and other organizations.

The total amount of educational work which is being done for and with our Spanish-speaking people is very large, and there is every reason for encouragement not only from the fact that for the most part educational opportunities are eagerly grasped after, but also because the Mexican has demonstrated the fact, beyond peradventure of disproval, that with adequate nourishment and under a favorable environment he has the ability to profit to the utmost from the very best educational opportunities which we can give him. And the very fact that mission schools charging tuition on the Border are filled to overflowing and are turning away hundreds of applicants every year for lack of room to accommodate them is but one of many circumstances which indicate the eagerness of both parents and children for the very best which we have to offer. Incidentally, in this connection, it would seem to be significant that in one boarding-school for Mexican pupils a set of "The Book of Knowledge" placed in the library of the school was almost worn out from constant use the first year.

CHAPTER VI

A FORWARD LOOK

"WILL they all go back to Mexico as soon as conditions become settled there?"

This question has been asked again and again, and is still being asked. What will happen when the Mexicans on the Border become reasonably assured that conditions in Mexico have become stabilized, that their lives and property will be safe back in the homeland, and that economic conditions have sufficiently improved to warrant the establishment of a home there.

So many unexpected things have happened in the days that have passed that no one but a prophet would be justified in making an authentic statement on this interesting point. Nevertheless, I venture the prediction that the last decade has ushered in for us an entirely new permanent situation so far as the Mexican in the United States is concerned. Many Mexicans will, of course, return to Mexico, but it is also to be expected that many other Mexicans will come to the United States. The stream which has been flowing so freely in the recent past has worn too smooth a channel to be suddenly checked unless very radical measures are taken to check it. Under present conditions the Mexican is eagerly welcomed in this country. Never did so many Mexicans have relatives and friends in the United States; never did they know so much about the United States as now, and it is perhaps

fair to believe that never before did they have such a
wholesome respect for our country and her institutions.
Our Committee on Public Information is said to have
done an extremely important piece of work in Mexico
during the War, and the Mexican people not only came
to understand what the War was all about, but they also
learned many things about the United States which they
had never before known.

In order to understand just what may be expected to
happen if conditions continue to improve in Mexico, we
should remind ourselves just who these people are who
are at present in our midst. Some of them are political
refugees who have no idea of staying permanently in the
United States. As soon as they are assured of personal
amnesty they will return to Mexico to look after their
financial and other interests there. Even some of these
political refugees have, during their period of waiting,
engaged in business in this country and formed so many
connections here that, although they may return to Mexico for a time or many times, the United States will be
the scene of most of their future activities. Then there
are the contract laborers who have been admitted under
special arrangement and who, by the very terms of their
admission, are supposed to be returned at the close of
their period of employment. The largest part of the
recent immigration, however, is made up of poor Mexicans who during the long period of revolution and ban-
ditry in Mexico have come to the United States in order
to find a place where their existence would be to some
extent more tolerable. Some have said that they have
suffered worse in America than they did in Mexico, but
for the most part they have found remunerative employment at wages many times those which they were receiv-

ing in Mexico, and they have found advantages for their children which are far superior to those which they were enjoying in Mexico. It is fair to assume that those who are established in the new land will think twice, or thrice, before they pack up and return to the uncertainties of Mexico. For those who have been admitted through the regular ports of entry there is always the danger that, should they again be dissatisfied with Mexico and desire to return to the United States, the stricter immigration regulations would prevent them from coming again to this country, and, for those who have come across the line without troubling to pass through a regular port of entry, there is the same danger. Then, too, enough Mexicans have come to the United States, so that none need to be lonely for the companionship of his fellow countrymen who can speak his language. Some one has pointed out that one out of ten of the Mexicans is already in the United States, and this is not far from the truth, if we include also the Spanish-Americans here. In other words, there never was greater reason for the Mexican to be content in the United States, and there are still many good reasons why he should hesitate to return to Mexico.

So far as the boys and girls who have been born and are being born in the United States and who are growing up, attending the public schools, and forming their early attachments here, there is no apppeal from Mexico as the homeland, since they are native sons and have their associations and their interests here. Many of these boys and girls would sooner or later return to the United States even if their parents should take them back to Mexico meantime. This fact alone would seem to make it certain that we have for all time to come materially increased our Mexican stock. Whether this will eventuate to our advantage or not will be determined very largely by our wisdom and our tact in dealing with certain very important problems in the days ahead.

Nowhere in the United States is the problem of Americanization a more complex one than here. Our non-English-speaking immigrants from nearly every other country come to us across thousands of miles of ocean. On the contrary, in our Southwest tens of thousands of Mexican immigrants live literally within the proverbial "stone's throw" of their native land. They can see it each day if they care to do so, and it is always "just across the line." They may live and die in the United States, but yet Mexico is there, and with all her faults they love her still. It is not surprising that few Mexicans apply for American citizenship, for Mexico is always a tantalizing possibility. We have, therefore, thousands of Mexicans in the United States who have no desire to become Americans or to be "Americanized," and they never expect to be. As fair-minded Americans we can either eject them bodily from the country or we can endeavor to be decent to them while they remain with us. In many cases their children are destined to be loyal American citizens, and possibly we can afford to be patient with them, if they are not overly eager to learn the English language or to take on American ways.

For many years to come, if not permanently, the Border must be a place of two languages, and the more Americans who understand Spanish and the more Mexicans who understand English the better it will be for all concerned. There is no better way for two nations to understand each other than for them to understand each other's language. There is every reason why the educational institutions on the American side of the Border should furnish every opportunity for English-speaking pupils to learn Spanish and for Spanish-speaking pupils to learn English, and Mexico in turn should provide similar opportunities on her side of the line. The matter is of sufficient importance to warrant some definite international understanding and method of procedure. In the meantime we should be patient and remind ourselves that "Americanization" which so often simmers down to the learning of the English language must, in many instances, in the very nature of the case move slowly.

It should be noted that we have been talking about Mexicans in the United States and not about Spanish-speaking American citizens. With this latter group there has been an excuse for their ignorance of English, but it is an excuse which cannot long remain valid, and vigorous measures should at once be taken to see to it that such educational steps are taken as will make it unnecessary for any commmunity in the United States, made up of native-born American citizens, to be dependent upon a foreign language for the transaction of its affairs or the carrying on of its social life.

The War has had its effect here, both upon the young men who went into the service and upon those who stayed at home, for a new patriotism was instilled, and the desire to learn the English language was quickened. How much this was needed is perhaps illustrated by the story told on good authority that native-born Spanish-speaking Americans claimed military exemption on the ground that they were not American citizens, and that this was done in all good faith and with no attempt to deceive. One of the by-products of the War, namely, the increased wages for common labor, has had a large and far-reaching effect upon Spanish-American towns of long standing. Some have for this reason lost from ten to sixty or seventy per cent of their population. The assumption is that as most of these people go out to larger centers or mingle more actively in the life of to-day they will learn and come to use the English language. During the War Work Campaign the Y. M. C. A. did a valuable piece of Americanization work on the Border. This included, among other things, the distribution of $40,000 worth of Spanish pamphlets and other propaganda work.

Now that the centuries-old seclusion of our Spanish Southwest is being broken up, it is not to be expected that opinions and attitudes will remain in the same static condition as in the past. Nor is it to be expected that our Spanish-speaking friends will be immune from harmful propaganda. Already there has been much I. W. W. and radical socialistic agitation fomented by Spanish-speaking agitators. This propaganda has been both against the church and the state. Dr. Vernon M. McCombs of Los Angeles describes a "cross-eyed, Spanish-speaking agitator haranguing some 200 Mexicans from a broken chair in the Plaza." The following poem and pledge was widely distributed as a part of this propaganda:

CHURCHES AND BIBLES

By Harry Hermann

The church is a fiend,
The Bible a lie,
Though Jesus and God
Are extolled to the sky.

The preachers will tell us of God they are sent,
But their speech does betray that for money they went;
They talk of that beautiful home in the sky,
While they know of a truth they are telling a lie.

Food, clothing and shelter they're after . . . O, well!
So they jump to the pulpit and talk of that hell:
'Tis marvelous, indeed, how the dupes they do work,
While themselves from all useful employment they shirk.

The time has now come
For the preacher to shun,
Put God and his Jesus to hell on the run;
The infidels, atheists, agnostics are here
To proclaim the glad tidings, a message of cheer.

So to hell with the churches, the bibles and all,
'Tis nothing but graft, and bitter as gall;
If worship you must, then worship a God
Who will give you a living without being a fraud.

Anti-Enlistment League

I ...., being
over eighteen years of age, hereby pledge myself against en-
listing as a volunteer in any military or naval service in
international war, offensive or defensive, and against giving
my approval to any enlistment on the part of others.

City..

State...

Street..

Date..

The foregoing is a sample of the character and spirit
of many tracts and cartoons which have been distributed
broadcast among the Mexicans of the Southwest. The
literature for this propaganda is not limited to tracts,
however; many books are used, such as "Jesus Christ
Never Existed," "Mary Magdalene, the Mistress of
Jesus," "An Imaginary God, the Child of Fear," and
others of like nature. How deeply the seeds of atheism
and radical socialism have been implanted up to date it is

difficult to say. The work has gone far enough, however, to warrant the undertaking of aggressive steps to counteract such harmful agiation. It is significant that a member of the Mexican national legislature returned, after a trip throughout the Southwest among Mexicans, to report in Mexico City that "the United States is becoming I. W. W. and atheistic." It is also significant that in the Bisbee deportation some time ago one-third were of Mexicans. The ignorance of the Mexicans makes a fertile field for the planting of all sorts of corrupting ideas and nothing but a counter-attack along lines of education, and the implanting of the Christian principles of individual responsibility for and service to the group will protect them from this insidious propaganda which is continually beng spread among them. Incidentally it must be noted, however, that education must be accompanied by a rigorous application of the principles of social justice to our treatment of the Mexican. Churches and schools and ministers and social workers are already doing much to counteract these dangerous tendencies which are manifesting themselves among the Mexicans, and this is done, not only through the general influence of the work; but also by direct dealing with unsafe leaders and agitators. Many of the fine and educated Mexican pastors are in a position to render and are rendering a unique service of this character among their fellow-countrymen, a service which one of another race could hardly perform.

The fact that Mexican labor has been largely engaged in agricultural projects where decentralization is the order of the day may account to some extent for the fact that we have not had more labor disturbances than we have had. Just what the future has in store along this line will be for us to determine, either by our foresightedness, or by our negligence and indifference. The Mexican in the United States is just finding himself. Some day he will be more conscious of his power and his importance than he is to-day. If we are discreet enough we shall see to it that these Mexicans in the United States are so fairly and decently treated that they will never have occasion to express their race consciousness or to act as a unit for the attainment of social justice. Up to date the Mexican has had many reasons for distrusting the disinterested motives of America and Americans, and these fears have been played upon by both priests and politicians. The mere fact that a Mexican has been forced to seek refuge in the United States does not of necessity imply that he has a very high regard for Americans. It is little short of amazing, however, to see how quickly this inbred distrust of America and Americans disappears before the sunlight of understanding, friendly sympathy, and kindly interest expressed by Americans who are eager to serve and to work with him rather than to exploit him.

So many aspects of the problem come back for their final solution to a question of the human elements involved that we are not likely to give the matter too much attention. If we insist upon assuming a mental and moral superiority to the Mexican, and upon looking at him as a convenient beast of burden, useful so long as he stays such, and undesirable as soon as he begins to elevate himself and his standard of living and to become our competitor in the various fields of activity which we like to look upon as distinctly the province of "Americans," then we are preparing for ourselves a problem for the future, the solution of which will be as long drawn out and as difficult as any we have ever faced. Nothing but the frank recognition of the Mexican on his own merits and the determination to give him a chance to make of himself as a man all that he can make will help us to avoid catastrophe here. The Mexican in the United States in contrast to any other alien group here has at hand a nation fifteen million strong which will not permanently tolerate, in silence, insults and mistreatment. It is foolish to argue as to whether the Mexican is equal to or superior in ability to the Anglo-Saxon. That is quite beside the point, which is whether we are going to permit the Mexican to go as far along the pathway of achievement as his ability will permit him to go. If we accept him on this basis, we have no occasion to fear the future, but on any other basis there are indeed dangers ahead.

While legally the Mexican in the United States is a "white man" (and incidentally many of them are as white as Anglo-Saxons), and his children are admitted to the public schools, and he is permitted to purchase a ticket and ride on any train on which a white man can ride, yet there is a tendency in too many quarters to insist that "A Mexican is a Mexican." There is no disposition on the part of the present writer to deny that fact; he might even say with equal enthusiasm that "An American is an American." Nor is there any question about the fact that there are some very bad Mexicans and that probably the percentage of dishonest Mexicans and of poverty-stricken Mexicans is greater than the percentage of similar classes among Americans. But to any student of the situation this would seem to indicate, not that the Mexican is born with any particular moral deficiency, but rather that he has unfortunately been cursed with a political and a religious environment which has been largely responsible for making him what he is. On the other hand, I know Mexicans who are as cultured and as thoroughly educated as the most fastidious American could desire for a friend; Mexicans who speak and read, not two languages alone, but three and four; Mexicans whose ideals of integrity and personal honor are on a par with the best Anglo-Saxon ideals; and Mexicans whose charming manners and sensitive natures make of them delightful companions and ornaments for any drawing-room. For an American to snub a Mexican because of his birth is for him to reveal his own provincialism and to cast a blot upon the fair name of America. Mr. S. G. Inman, in "Intervention in Mexico," tells of an American coming to the end of a trip as a guest of Mexican officials and business men in Mexico during which he, with other Americans, had been shown something of the marvelous resources of Mexico, and had been entertained by some of the most cultured and most prosperous people in Mexico and in a style of which Americans need not have been ashamed, remarking in the presence of Mexicans, and even before he had crossed the international line, "There are two things I could never understand, why the Lord made mosquitoes and Mexicans." Such an exhibition of incivility, discourtesy, and absolute foolishness is not only un-American, but it is also un-Mexican, for even the humblest Mexican can teach us many things about the art of politeness. The incident, however, is more than an isolated incident, it is but an illustration of an attitude of assumed superiority of one race over another, and an attitude which can only bring disaster in our dealings with the Mexican, if we persist in it or permit the unthinking element of our population to give frequent expression to it.

Fortunately there is every reason to believe that the conditions which make for a continuance of this attitude are rapidly passing away. There is a steadily growing respect for America and Americans on the part of Mexico, and there is a similarly enhanced respect for Mexico and Mexicans being developed among Americans. Whatever President Obregon may have said or thought about Americans in the past, his regard for them has been steadily increasing as he has come to know them better. He frankly recognizes the large part which American capital has played and must continue to play in the development of Mexico; he has declared that the foreign debts of the Mexican republic will be paid; and he has very plainly declared his conviction that friendship with the United States is not only essential to Mexican progress, but that it will be the aim of his government to promote such friendship. All of this augurs well, not only for the future relationships of the two governments concerned, but also for the future relationships of the two races concerned.

As these words are being written word comes that in line with the previous declaration of the Obregon government to establish a "dry zone" on the Border one of the very worst resorts there, namely, the "Owl," at Mexicali has been closed by order of the new government in Lower California. If a similar policy is followed along the entire Border, one of the greatest occasions of misjudgment of each other may be done away, for it was here on the international line where the very worst elements of Mexico and the United States met and where respect for each other was lost in the free reign of vice. If we can now supplement this very necessary and desirable negative program with a positive program which will supply wholesome interests and activities for those which have long been so extremely unwholesome, we may as a nation breathe a freer and purer atmosphere in the future than we have in the past along our extended southern Border.

It is apparent long before this that, try as we will to limit our attention to those phases of the Mexican question which lie north of the international line, we continually find ourselves dipping down into Old Mexico herself. It is suggestive of the fundamentally artificial character of our political demarcations and of the insistence of human nature in disregarding them. We can as little permanently confine people and social problems within political areas as we can control water with a basket; they will not stay "put." Mexico's problems and Mexico's achievements become ours by the very law of propinquity, and the rapidity and extent of our progress is to a very considerable extent conditioned by hers. We have more than a mere neighborly interest, therefore, in Mexico's progress educationally, socially, and economically. We are man and wife by common law marriage, and no international divorce court can ever issue a decree which will separate our interests.

Not only should we understand each other's language, but we should also understand each other's history, traditions, and customs. Many who cannot learn another language or who would have little occasion to use it can at least take pains to be informed about these neighbors who are not destined to move soon out of the neighborhood. A little study of the historical background for the situation to be found in the Southwest will not only put us into a more intelligent touch with the Mexicans themselves, but it will also give us a more sympathetic understanding of our own Spanish-American fellow citizens. For many who are removed from personal contact with these people, an understanding of the situation and a loyal support of the agencies dealing with them is perhaps all that can be expected; for those who live in intimate contact with it duty does not end there. The whole nation has a right to expect that every true American who has dealings with an individual of Mexican origin shall maintain an attitude of friendliness and respect toward him, and treat him with all the fairness and the justice which he would accord to one of another race. To do less is not only to bring reproach upon America but to lay up for all of us serious complications for the future.

We have a difficult task to perform; it is the ever complicated one of endeavoring to help a people who are in need without doing them more harm than good, without pauperizing them as we try to assist them. Both the Mexican in the United States and the Spanish-American have needs deep and far-reaching which we must from all the motives of altruism and self-interest help to meet. These needs are physical, economic, intellectual, moral, and spiritual. We cannot refuse to meet them without great danger to ourselves. The Mexican in our national life has become too numerous to ignore; he is too important a factor in our life to forget; but as we assist him to take his place as an integral part of our body politic, and not as an alien adjunct thereto, we must endeavor to master the fine art of working *with* and not so exclusively *for* him as we have in the past. In the accomplishment of this task we ought to be able to call into play the best efforts of some of the best educated, most cultured, and wealthiest Mexicans in our midst. If they have not been accustomed to engage in altruistic tasks, they ought to be trained to do so. At present there is too great a gulf fixed between the more fortunate and the poorer Mexican in the United States. There seems to be no medium through which the one can help the other. We have been so impressed at times with the needs of the poorer Mexican that we have not only ignored the needs of the more prosperous, but we have also failed to bring the resources of the one to the help of the other to their mutual advantage.

A gentleman of Mexican extraction has suggested in this connection that we need in important centers more "Mexican Centers," institutions which will furnish a meeting place for people of Mexican extraction, not a social settlement for the poor and in which a more fortunate Mexican would hesitate to be seen, but centers so conducted as to bring no social reproach upon those who enter their walls but rather to serve as the nucleus of the Mexican life of the community and of an educational and social program which will interest and minister to groups of many sorts. Something of this sort has already been achieved in certain centers opened by the Y. W. C. A., the Y. M. C. A., certain churches, and other agencies; but only a beginning has been made, and we are still in the class of learners.

Of course there is no one solution to a problem so large, so diversified, and so complex. It will require the best efforts of all of us applied in many ways and through many channels. The essential thing is for us to recognize that the Mexican is with us to stay, that our future is inextricably bound up with his, as with no other alien race, that we must live together whether we will or no, and, most important of all, that the Mexican is a *man* with fine, sensitive qualities of nature and with capabilities which are destined to lead him, no one knows how far, along the path of progress. He is a factor to be reckoned with, but to be reckoned with gladly, for he comes bringing gifts; and his already large and steadily increasing contribution to our life is helping to make America a better place in which to live and a far more interesting abode because of the rich and diversified endowments which he brings with him.

Our great Southwest, destined to be the chief amphitheater of the Mex-American life in our country, is already an empire in itself, but its marvelous resources have only begun to be exploited. Within the last decade hundreds of thousands of acres of what was once supposed to be permanent desert have been transformed into veritable garden spots, and millions of dollars worth of products are being produced where nothing but cactus and sagebrush had ever grown before. Dams have been built, irrigation projects opened, and electric power plants erected. Great pumping outfits have been established, and these are increasing as the water power is more thoroughly harnessed, so that land which could not otherwise be watered may have water pumped for its use. Thus everywhere the thirsty desert is being transformed and the Mexican is making this transformation possible. He does not limit his activities to the surface of the ground, however, for he is a natural miner, and he may be found underground or digging into the side of a mountain to release the hidden coal, gold, silver, copper, and other minerals with which the hills of the Southwest are stored.

We have heard a great deal in recent years about "city planning." Once people let their cities grow up as chance might dictate, and then one day they woke to the folly of such a procedure. Why not plan the city in advance, and thus direct the lines of its growth so that the final result might be more pleasing to the eye and more worthy of the people to whom it belonged? To-day we are as a nation building a great empire in our Southwest, and we are building it, to a large extent, out of stones quarried from the human quarries of Old Mexico. Up to date we have moved ahead without much plan and with slight vision of what the final result might chance to be. Is it not time that we should begin to consider with care what we are building in order that the product of the formative years just ahead may be pleasing to behold and may be worthy of a great nation established upon principles of justice, enlightenment, and human brotherhood?

Among those who have been wise enough to see and plan for the future is the Mormon Church. In the very center of the Southwest in the Salt River Valley of Arizona which has risen almost overnight from the wilderness and clothed itself with verdure of remarkable beauty and economic value, the Mormons have quietly established themselves on thousands of acres of the most productive soil. They have reared their neat chapels, and now they have projected a Mormon Temple to cost at least $600,000. This will make the Salt River Valley the great Mormon center of the Southwest, and from it will go out scores of missionaries to work among Mexicans both above and below the Border. Already many adherents of Mormonism are reported in Old Mexico, in Sonora, Chihuahua, and other states, and a recent report indicates thirty-seven Spanish-speaking Mormon missionaries in the four states of Arizona, New Mexico, Texas, and Colorado. It is reported that a considerable number of Mexican converts to Mormonism in the United States have already been baptized.

It is for the people of America to determine whether the ideals of Mormonism, of the I. W. W., of radical socialism, of atheism, and infidelity, or of the very best that America has to offer are to dominate the Southwest which is to-day in the making. Possibly nowhere else has America an opportunity, at the moment, to do a finer, more constructive and more rewarding bit of national prophylaxis than here.

A word to the wise is sufficient.

THE END

COST OF LIVING STUDIES. V

HOW MEXICANS EARN AND LIVE

A STUDY OF THE INCOMES AND EXPENDITURES
OF ONE HUNDRED MEXICAN FAMILIES
IN SAN DIEGO, CALIFORNIA

BY

THE HELLER COMMITTEE FOR RESEARCH IN SOCIAL ECONOMICS
OF THE UNIVERSITY OF CALIFORNIA

AND

CONSTANTINE PANUNZIO

University of California Publications in Economics
Volume 13, No. 1, pp. 1–114
Issued May 17, 1933

University of California Press
Berkeley, California

————

Cambridge University Press
London, England

CONTENTS

APPENDICES

LIST OF TABLES

FOREWORD

THE STUDY HEREWITH PRESENTED, though primarily a cost of living study, is perhaps most interesting if regarded as a study in national adjustment.

According to current ways of thinking, the principle of nationalism is one of the fundamental guides to life. Every nation has its particular form of nationalism, and strangers coming to a new land are today inevitably called on to adjust themselves to the forms of life that taken together constitute the "nationalism" they find about them.

The adjustment may result from a desire on the part of the immigrant to fit in, or from insistence on the part of those who are living according to the national standards. The motive is not here in question. The point is that immigrants must and do adjust.

Such an adjustment is plainly evident in this study of one hundred Mexican families. According to those who have been in Mexico, Mexican ways of living, especially those of the mass of the working class, differ greatly from the ways of living in the United States. Whether they differ to the advantage of the Mexican or to that of the American living in the United States depends on the point of view of the investigator. The one consideration here is the fact of difference. These one hundred families, whose earnings and spendings are given in detail, show the habits of living of a group not yet wholly adjusted to the American standard. The food consumption of these families still tends to resemble strongly that of the land from which they came. As to the use of other forms of consumer's goods, each category plainly shows the families being subjected in varying degrees to the new conditions of economic life in which they find themselves.

Because Mexicans are among our latest comers, and because they are a source of special interest in that they are late comers, the cost of living study contained in the ensuing pages should mean a contribution to more than facts about the cost of living. In addition, it pictures the ways of living of a national group of recent arrivals. It is hoped that those who study the tables, which give plainly and exactly what these families earned and how they spent what they earned, will also find less specifically set forth certain facts that will help tell a story of the adjustments that take place as new peoples come slowly but surely under the influence of our national life.

JESSICA B. PEIXOTTO, *Chairman,*

Heller Committee for Research in Social Economics

BERKELEY, CALIFORNIA

ACKNOWLEDGMENTS

THE AUTHORS of this study have many acknowledgments to make. Through the good offices of Dr. Paul S. Taylor, of the University of California, Professor Panunzio and the Heller Committee were enabled to plan and carry out the study as a joint undertaking. The Board of Directors of San Diego Neighborhood House made it possible for Professor Panunzio, then Director of the House, to take charge of the investigation and for the staff to conduct the actual field work. In addition, the Board of Directors contributed about one-half the cost of the field work. The rest was contributed by Professor and Mrs. Panunzio. Acknowledgment is due also to the Board of Education of the San Diego City Schools, and in particular to Superintendent Walter S. Hepner, who made the services of some of the Immigrant Education teachers available for the field work. Mrs. Lenore Panunzio, at that time Supervisor of Immigrant Education for the city schools, secured this cooperation. Special mention should be made of Miss Marian Branson, home teacher in the city schools, and Mrs. Grace Jacques, a member of the staff at Neighborhood House, who did the major part of the field work. The patience and skill of the investigators and the cheerful cooperation of the Mexican families themselves in the face of a prolonged and tedious inquiry deserve grateful mention.

The preparation of this study has been shared between the joint authors. The study was initiated and the field investigation in San Diego was directed by Professor Panunzio. The schedule and technique of the study were adapted from the form used by the Heller Committee in earlier investigations. The Heller Committee analyzed the findings and, in collaboration with Professor Panunzio, has prepared them for publication.

HOW MEXICANS EARN AND LIVE

A STUDY OF THE INCOMES AND EXPENDITURES OF ONE
HUNDRED MEXICAN FAMILIES IN SAN DIEGO,
CALIFORNIA

BY

THE HELLER COMMITTEE FOR RESEARCH IN SOCIAL ECONOMICS
OF THE UNIVERSITY OF CALIFORNIA
AND
CONSTANTINE PANUNZIO

I

INTRODUCTORY

FOR THE PAST THREE OR FOUR DECADES, Mexican immigration
to the United States has brought out two sharply contrasted
views concerning the Mexican. On the one hand, the Mexican's racial and cultural background, his capacity for work, his
standard of living, his adaptability to our institutions have all been
subjected to hostile criticism. On the other hand, he has been ac-
claimed as an admirable and competent addition to the low-scale
wage group regarded as an integral part of economic progress. The
group that criticizes makes itself very audible. Organized labor
opposes the Mexican chiefly as a competitor of the American
laborer. He is accused of a tendency to take wages below the minimum standard set by trade unions. Social workers for the most part
see in the Mexicans an addition to the population which adds large
numbers to the indigents in any community where they settle.
Employers look at the matter differently. For them the Mexican is
a necessary adjunct of the present labor supply in the United
States. His are the hands which are ready to do the spade work.

Both points of view are based on armchair observations or practical day-to-day experience, rather than on studies of facts. Since 1929 a series of ordered observations has been published, adding facts to these opinions. Of first importance are the field studies of Dr. Paul S. Taylor of the University of California, nine monographs (1929–1933) on *Mexican Labor in the United States*. This series of investigations gives·many and valuable data about the life and labor of the Mexican. The scholarly detachment that characterizes the presentation of the material adds weight and conviction. Governor C. C. Young's Fact-Finding Committee's Report, *Mexicans in California* (1930), is another source of new information. Two studies by Dr. Manuel Gamio, *Mexican Immigration to the United States* (1930) and *The Mexican Immigrant* (1931), also help to throw light on certain major aspects in the life of the Mexican. Together these studies answer questions such as the following: Are the Mexicans actually needed as laborers? Do they receive wages commensurate with the work they do in a given community? Are the wages they receive adequate to meet their cost of living? Are they, relatively speaking, a good social element in the community?

The study contained in the following pages answers those questions particularly relating to the cost of living. A detailed picture is given of the ways of spending of one hundred Mexican non-migratory, wage-earning families residing in a Mexican neighborhood in 1929–1930. Whether the group is typical is matter for question. The families studied lived in the city of San Diego. They are a sample of the Mexican wage-earning population of California. To say that they are a typical and representative sample of the Mexican wage-earning group in the United States or in the State would be to add a guess to certainties.

A few facts concerning the Mexican population in California may give the group a further statistical setting. The restrictive immigration laws of 1921 and 1924, greatly reducing as they did the supply of low-skilled labor from southern and eastern Europe, brought in the Mexican, who was unaffected by these laws. The proportion of Mexicans in the total immigration into the United States rose from 3.8 per cent in the fiscal years 1911–1921 to 18.8 per cent in the year

ended June 30, 1928.[1] In 1930 there were 1,422,533 Mexicans in the
United States.[2] Because of the change in classification it is impossible to make a direct comparison with the number reported in
1920, but it seems fair to estimate the increase in the number of
Mexicans in these ten years as more than 100 per cent, whereas
the total population of the United States increased only 16 per cent
in this period. In 1930, Mexicans constituted 1.2 per cent of the
total population of the United States; of this number, 26 per cent
were in California. Census figures show that there were 368,013
Mexicans in California, constituting 6.5 per cent of the State's total
population. Within the State the major part of the Mexicans were
concentrated in the ten southern counties of Imperial, Kern, Los
Angeles, Orange, Riverside, Santa Barbara, San Bernardino, San
Diego, San Luis Obispo, and Ventura. In 1930 these counties had
a population of 3,044,978, or 53.6 per cent of the total population
of the State. In this population were 291,401 Mexicans, 79.2 per
cent of all the Mexicans in California. The average proportion of
Mexicans to total population in these ten counties was 9.6 per cent.
In Imperial County it rose to 35 per cent, in Ventura to 25 per cent.
The Mexicans are more concentrated in the rural districts than in
large cities. In California cities of 25,000 and over, the proportion
of Mexicans to total population in 1930 was 5.4 per cent; in the
remainder of the State it was 7.8 per cent. Recent years have shown
a tendency for Mexicans to move into the cities,[3] but 52.5 per cent
of the Mexicans in California in 1930 were in rural districts or
towns of less than 25,000 population.

The facts of population had very little to do with the choice of
San Diego as the location for the study herewith presented. Rather,
the city was chosen because Professor Panunzio was at that time
Director of San Diego Neighborhood House, a philanthropic enterprise in the Mexican district. The group of families included in this
study was not, therefore, necessarily typical of the average Mexican
family in California. These families were residents of one of the five

---

[1] *Mexicans in California*, 19–20. This figure includes only those legally
admitted.
[2] Fifteenth Census of the United States (1930).
[3] *Mexicans in California*, 57.

cities in the State with more than 100,000 population. Thus, automatically, all agricultural and migratory workers were excluded from the study. In 1930, 2.5 per cent of all Mexicans in California lived in San Diego, whose total population of 147,995 contained 9,266 Mexicans, 6.3 per cent of the population.

Mexicans live in San Diego under conditions that are, possibly, more than usually favorable. Most of them are in the southwestern portion of the city along the waterfront close to the factories and canneries. The streets are wide; sanitation is moderately good. Mexican stores, churches, pool halls, and the Neighborhood House are a part of the district. Living conditions are reasonably good. There is little or no serious congestion. The cottage type of house prevails. There are no slum tenements.

As Dr. Gamio has pointed out,[4] the mode of living of the Mexican workman who has become a resident of the United States naturally changes. If the following study is of value, it will show, first, the detail of this divergence between the Mexican's standard of living in this country and his standard of living at home, and, secondly, the divergence between the Mexican immigrant standard and the American standard. Mexicans on the whole retain the food habits of their own country, but they tend to adopt American clothing, and their housing conditions show a great improvement over those prevailing in Mexico.

The data presented in the following study, then, represent a sample of the Mexican settled in a moderately large city in California, who as a wage earner or small tradesman is adjusting himself with a larger income to a way of spending which is partly that which he brought from his own land and partly that of the land in which he lives.

In order that the group of families studied should be as homogeneous as possible, certain qualifications were set up: (1) One of the parents must be Mexican.[5] (2) The family must have been

---

[4] *Mexican immigration to the United States*, 140–147.

[5] In the Census of 1930 persons of Mexican birth or parentage who were not definitely returned as white or Indian were designated "Mexican." The same rule has been followed in the present study, so that "Mexican" implies race and not birthplace.

resident in San Diego for the twelve months preceding the investigation. (3) Both parents must be alive and at home. (4) The family
must include at least one child.

As is usual in such studies, the families were in the main self-
supporting and independent. Families were included, however,
which received free medical care—the almost universal resource of
the low-paid wage earner, gifts of clothing from an organization
like the Parent-Teachers' Association, or milk free or at reduced
rates from a milk station.

The study was designed to comprise only wage earners in the
strict sense of the term; but the investigators included families of
similar social and economic status in which the man was the pro-
prietor of a small business, earning no more than the average
skilled laborer, or a salaried clerk. The final group may, therefore,
be more truly described as the "low-income" class than as the
"wage-earning" class.

The information collected from these families included full
details about source and amount of income, items of expenditure,
and surplus or deficit, of the preceding twelve months. In addition,
certain special and identifying data were gathered, concerning
housing conditions, and the degree of dependency, age, sex, and
birthplace of every member of the household.[6]

The information was gathered in the summer of 1930. The
investigators were members of the staff of Neighborhood House,
San Diego, of which Professor Panunzio was then Director, and
teachers of adult classes in English in the city school system. The
families visited were either personally known to the investigator
or were neighbors or relatives of families already included.

As has been said, the final study explains the way of living of
100 families. Twenty-two additional schedules were discarded,
usually because of an unexplained discrepancy greater than 10
per cent between income and expenditure; occasionally because a
family was obviously of a higher economic level, or because of

---

[6] A similar schedule was published in a previous Heller Committee report,
Spending ways of a semi-skilled group, University of California Publications
in Economics, 5 (1931): 295–366. Copies of the schedule used in the present
study may be obtained from the Heller Committee.

refusal to give certain necessary information. The resources available for field work and compilation set the limit at 100 completed schedules. Statistically, this should be an adequate sample of a fairly homogeneous group.

Within the limits of the qualifications just noted, every attempt was made to secure an unbiased sample. Of course, in all studies of this kind the voluntary self-selection of the families which were willing to cooperate and the difficulties of recalling details of income and expenditure with the requisite accuracy are likely to single out the more intelligent and thrifty.

II

SOCIAL DATA

Composition of household.—The character of the group was determined by the qualifications set up for inclusion in the study. Thus there were a husband and a wife in each family, and at least one child. The average family had between three and four children. In a few families there were other relatives; two households included lodgers.[7]

TABLE 1

COMPOSITION OF HOUSEHOLD*

Members of household	Total number of persons in the group	Number of families containing such persons
All persons	600	100
Members of family*	558	100
Husbands†	100	100
Wives	100	100
Children	358	100
Relatives	40	27
Lodgers	2	2

* "Family" includes only parents and children. "Household" includes all members of family, all relatives living in the house, and lodgers.

† Two of these husbands were working away from home at the end of the study.

Nativity.—Ninety-one per cent of the parents and only 28 per cent of the children were natives of Mexico. Of the 271 persons born in the United States, all but two were born in California or the Southwest, the great majority in the former. Sixteen families included one American-born parent; ninety-one had at least one American-born child, and in over half the families all the children were born in the United States.

[7] Composition of household, ages, and housing conditions are reported for the date of the investigator's visit, ignoring variations at other periods of the year.

TABLE 2

BIRTHPLACE OF MEMBERS OF THE FAMILIES

Country of birth	All persons in family		Parents				Children	
			Fathers		Mothers			
	Number	Percentage	Number	Percentage	Number	Percentage	Number	Percentage
Total............................	558	....	100	....	100	....	358	....
Not reported..............	10	....	2	....	2	....	6	....
Total reported...........	548	100.0	98	100.0	98	100.0	352	100.0
Born in United States	271	49.5	6	6.1	12	12.2	253	71.9
Born in Mexico..........	277	50.5	92	93.9	86	87.8	99	28.1

Age of husbands and wives.—The requirement that each family should contain one child living at home limited the group so that

TABLE 3

AGE OF HUSBANDS AND WIVES

Age	Husbands		Wives	
	Number	Percentage	Number	Percentage
All ages............................	100	....	100	....
Not reported..................	1	....	1	....
Total reported...............	99	100.0	99	100.0
20–24................................	2	2.0	15	15.2
25–29................................	17	17.2	25	25.3
30–34................................	15	15.2	20	20.2
35–39................................	17	17.2	19	19.2
40–44................................	17	17.2	12	12.1
45–49................................	22	22.2	5	5.0
50–54................................	4	4.0	2	2.0
55–59................................	4	4.0	1	1.0
60–64................................	1	1.0	....	....
Average				
Mean................................	38.9 years		32.8 years	
Median............................	38.0 years		31.0 years	

few of the parents were either very young or elderly. Very few of
the men were under twenty-five years of age, or over fifty. Nearly
half the wives were between twenty-five and thirty-five; few were
over forty-five.

Children at home.—The 100 families had 358 children living at
home at the time of the investigation.[8] Nearly half the families
had either three or four children; only four families had more than
six. Exactly half the children were boys.

TABLE 4

NUMBER OF CHILDREN LIVING AT HOME PER FAMILY

Number of children	Number of families having specified number of children	
	All children	Dependent and semi-dependent* children
Total	100	100
None	....	....
One	16	16
Two	14	16
Three	20	22
Four	22	22
Five	12	11
Six	12	10
Seven	1	1
Eight	1	1
Nine	1	....
Ten	1	1
Average		
Mean	3.6	3.4
Median	3.5	3.3

* That is, earning less than 85 per cent of their cost of maintenance.

Most of the children were of school age or younger. Thirty-eight
per cent were less than six years old. Nearly three-fourths were
under eleven, and only 10 per cent were sixteen years or older. Of

[8] Children living away from home are not included in this study.

the latter group, only six—two boys and four girls—were over twenty-one. The typical family was thus composed of young children, dependent on the father's earnings. Only one family in five had a child old enough to be legally self-supporting, and these were generally the larger families with an unusual number of younger children.

TABLE 5

AGE OF CHILDREN AT LAST BIRTHDAY

Age	Number	Percentage
All ages	358	100.0
Less than 6	135	37.7
6–10	118	33.0
11–15	70	19.5
16–20	29	8.1
21 and over	6	1.7
Average		
Mean		7.9 years
Median		7.5 years

Other relatives.—Twenty-seven households included one or more relatives,[9] sometimes temporary visitors, sometimes permanent members of the family. Twenty-one of the forty relatives were wholly or partly supported by the family during the time they were in the home. The dependent relatives were usually the grandparents.

Boarders and lodgers.—In comparison with other working-class groups it seems surprising that only two families reported lodgers at the time the study was made, and that the only boarders were three men who roomed elsewhere but took their meals with the family. A procedure more common than taking lodgers was to rent a part of the house as a flat or as light-housekeeping rooms.

Occupations.—The majority of Mexican immigrants in this country are either agricultural laborers, usually migratory, or laborers

---

[9] Status at time of investigator's visit; nine others reported relatives in the household at some previous time in the year.

engaged in low-skilled industrial occupations. It is not surprising, therefore, to find half the men in this study in occupations classified as "low skilled"[10] and twenty more in semi-skilled work. The former group included twenty-five day laborers, ten cement workers, eight maintenance of way men, and seven men engaged at miscellaneous jobs requiring little or no ability or training. The semi-skilled group included such occupations as gardeners, pantrymen, truck drivers, firemen, janitors. Fifteen were skilled workmen, including a carpenter, a plasterer, a meat cutter, a blacksmith, foremen, cooks, and tailors. In addition to the wage earners there were five men with "white collar" jobs as salesmen, agents, or shop clerks; seven small tradesmen, including a contractor, a tailor, a cobbler, two proprietors of barber shops, and the owners of a fishing boat and of a tortilla factory. One minister represented the professions. Two men were too old or ill to work.

Nearly half the women, forty-four, were gainfully occupied at some time in the year, but their work in most cases was limited to irregular, part-time employment, undertaken to supplement the family income, rather than a customary, full-time job. Of the forty-four women, thirty-two worked in canneries at cleaning and packing fish. Four of them worked full time during part of the year; the others worked broken time. In no case did the canneries provide full-time, year-round jobs. The only woman reporting fifty-two weeks of steady work had an invalid husband and was employed in a laundry. Five women worked as shop clerks, four of them for thirty weeks or more. Two other women worked in laundries; one was a cigar maker and one an office worker for brief periods; one did sewing; one assisted in her husband's store without pay.

Since the great majority of the children were still young, it is natural that but few of them were gainfully employed. Children from the age of eleven onward earned small sums out of school hours. The youngest self-supporting child with a regular, full-time

---

[10] The classification of occupations in the accompanying table can only be suggestive, certainly not final. No satisfactory classification of occupations according to degree of skill is available, and the traditional classification by industry, following the Census, fails to reflect the social and economic status of the worker in his community, which is our chief interest in the present study.

TABLE 6

Occupations of Men and Women*

Occupation†	Men	Women
Total	100	100
None	2	56‡
I. Professional and executive	*1*	....
Minister	1	....
II. "White collar" jobs	*12*	*7*
Small tradesmen	7	....
Salesmen and agents	3	....
Clerical workers	....	1
Shop assistants	2	6¶
III. Skilled workmen	*15*	*1*
Foremen	3	....
Cleaners	2	....
Tailors	2	....
Cooks	2	....
Others	6	1
IV. Semi-skilled workers	*20*	*36*
Cannery operatives	....	32
Kitchen and pantry workers	4	....
Gardeners	3	....
Taxi and truck drivers	3	....
Firemen	2	....
Lumber assorters	2	....
Laundry operatives	....	3
Others	6	1
V. Low-skilled workers	*50*	....
Day laborers	25	....
Gas company	6	
Street-car company	2	....
Cannery	3	....
Odd jobs	4	....
Not specified	3	....
Miscellaneous	7	....
Cement workers	10	....
Maintenance of way laborers	8	....
Others	7	....

* Persons engaged in more than one occupation within the year were classified under that in which they spent the longest time.

† Classification modified from Taussig, *Principles of Economics*, II: 134–137, 1913 ed.

‡ Housewives.

¶ Includes one woman who helped in her husband's shop without pay.

job was seventeen years old. The school children sold papers and junk, ran errands, did odd jobs, or were mothers' helpers. The children of legal working age who were still partly dependent upon their parents, were usually working irregularly in the canneries or laundries, at caddying, or in domestic service. The older, independent ones with full-time work were engaged in much the same occupations as their parents. Four of the six self-supporting girls worked in canneries, one did housework, and one was a waitress. The eight independent boys included a timekeeper and a laborer in the canneries, a mechanic's helper, a cleaner and dyer, a car cleaner, and a laundryman.

INCOME

"Income" includes all cash receipts during the year that went into the current family fund, with the exception of money borrowed or drawn from savings. The latter items represent a deficit.[11] Money earned by the children and not contributed to the general family fund[12] was not included, unless the expenses for which it was dis-

TABLE 7

AMOUNT OF TOTAL FAMILY INCOME DURING THE YEAR

Total annual income	Number of families	Percentage of all families
All amounts	100	100.0
Less than $250.00	1	1.0
$250.00–$499.99	2	2.0
500.00– 749.99	6	6.0
750.00– 999.99	13	13.0
1000.00–1249.99	22	22.0
1250.00–1499.99	23	23.0
1500.00–1749.99	16	16.0
1750.00–1999.99	8	8.0
2000.00–2249.99	6	6.0
2250.00–2499.99	2	2.0
2500.00–2749.99	1	1.0

Average	
Mean	$1337.35
Median	1273.75

bursed, such as clothes, were also reported and included in the budget. Accordingly, "income from children" or "from relatives" applies only to their contributions, not to their total earnings.

[11] In this study the problem of money transferred from one investment to another within the year did not arise.

[12] Nineteen of the thirty-nine working children retained part of their earnings and refused to report how these sums were spent.

In ninety of the 100 families the cash income was supplemented by income in kind from one or more sources, usually home-grown food or culls from the markets, firewood gathered along the beach or tracks, gifts of second-hand clothing, or free medical care. The difficulties of expressing the value of second-hand shoes or clinic care in terms of dollars and cents made it impossible to include such items in the cash total.

Amount of total incomes.—The total annual family income varied from $156.20 in a family where the man had only five weeks' work in the year and the deficit was made up from savings, to $2500 earned by a contracting brick-mason. The average family income was about $100 a month   ($1337.35 per year mean, $1273.75 median). Forty-five per cent of the families reported total incomes between $1000 and $1500, and three-fourths reported between $750 and $1750.

TABLE 8

AMOUNT AND PERCENTAGE OF ANNUAL INCOME FROM SPECIFIED SOURCES

Sources of income	Number of families reporting	Average annual income for families reporting			
		Mean		Median	
		Amount	Per-centage	Amount	Per-centage
Total income	100	$1337.35	100.0	$1273.75	100.0
Man's earnings	98	1085.41	80.6	1060.25	82.5
Income from other sources	76	360.07	26.7	240.00	18.7
Wife's earnings	43	276.50	20.9	216.00	17.1
Children's contributions	16	502.71	35.2	422.50	29.5
From relatives	22	209.29	15.2	209.00	16.4
In household	15	245.30	18.1	240.00	18.9
Elsewhere	8	115.62	8.1	65.00	4.5
Boarders and lodgers	6	87.02	6.5	55.50	4.4
Property	7*	162.75	10.6	84.00	5.5
Insurance	3	217.67	12.9	49.00	2.8
Pension from Mexico	1	160.00	28.0	180.00	28.0
Other	8	41.69	3.5	40.00	3.3

* Includes one family which sub-let four housekeeping rooms at no net gain.

Sources of income.—About 80 per cent of the average family's income was derived from the man's earnings. The rest of the family income came chiefly from the earnings of wife, children, and relatives living in the household. An occasional family received income from boarders or lodgers, rent from property—a house owned elsewhere, a garage, housekeeping rooms, flats in their own dwelling—gifts of money from relatives outside the household, payments from insurance policies, a pension from Mexico, a repaid loan, or the sale of various possessions, such as a car, a baby buggy, chickens, or jewelry.

TABLE 9

AMOUNT OF MAN'S EARNINGS DURING THE YEAR

Annual earnings	Number of families	Percentage of all families
All amounts......................................	98	100.0
Less than $250.00............................	3	3.1
$250.00–$499.99...............................	6	6.1
500.00– 749.99...............................	9	9.2
750.00– 999.99...............................	24	24.5
1000.00–1249.99...............................	27	27.5
1250.00–1499.99...............................	13	13.3
1500.00–1749.99...............................	10	10.2
1750.00–1999.99...............................	4	4.1
2000.00–2249.99...............................	1	1.0
2250.00–2499.99...............................	....	....
2500.00–2749.99...............................	1	1.0

Average	
Mean......................................	$1085.41
Median...................................	1060.25

Men's earnings.—The average man in these families earned a trifle over $1000 a year ($1085.41 mean, $1060.25 median).[13] Half the men earned between $750 and $1250. Such low earning capacity was to be expected in view of the occupations in which they were engaged. Considering the general grade of skill, there was less

[13] The Census of Manufacturers, 1929 (Mimeo. release, May 11, 1931) reports the average number of wage earners in San Diego as 3,859, the yearly wage bill as $5,258,177, or average annual earnings of $1363 per wage earner in manufacturing industries.

unemployment than might perhaps have been expected. Fifty-three men worked full-time for fifty weeks or more in the year; seventy-eight were employed for at least three-fourths of the year. In two families the man was an invalid, and the mother or son the chief wage earner.

Women's earnings.—Forty-three women added to the family income of the year.[14] On the whole, these women were working in order to supplement inadequate incomes from other sources, since, with their earnings included, the average income in these families was no larger than in families where the woman did not work. The average yearly earnings of their husbands were $300 lower than in the other fifty-seven families.

The irregular character of the women's employment has already been discussed (page 11). Their average earnings were small, less than $20 a month ($276.50 per year mean, $216 median). Twelve of the forty-three earned less than $100 in the year. Eight, including the five full-time employees who worked more than six months, earned between $500 and $950.

Children's earnings.—Only sixteen families received income from children's earnings; in eight others the children earned small sums for pocket-money or clothes, but contributed nothing to the general family fund. Consequently working children were not an important factor in the income of the group as a whole, income from this source averaging only $80 per year per family for the 100 families. In the families where children were working, however, the average return was high ($502.71 mean, $422.50 median). In two families where more than one child was working, income from this source amounted to $1300 and $1600. The largest single contribution was $950 from one girl of twenty-three, who turned over her entire earnings to her mother. Of the thirty-nine working children, twenty turned over all their earnings and nineteen kept some for spending money, in which case the mother usually did not know the child's total earnings. There appeared to be no difference in the practice of boys and girls in this regard.

---

[14] Another woman worked in the family store, but received no regular wages.

Comparison of the children's earnings with their actual costs of maintenance shows that, of the 358 children, 318, or 88.8 per cent, were totally dependent; 24, 6.7 per cent, earned less than 85 per

TABLE 10

STATUS OF DEPENDENCY OF CHILDREN, CLASSIFIED BY AGE

Status of dependency*	Age of children					
	All ages	Less than 6	6 to 10	11 to 15	16 to 20	21 and over
Number						
Total	358	135	118	70	29	6
Dependent	*342*	*135*	*118*	*70*	*17*	*2*
Totally	318	135	118	59	6	......
Partially	24	......	......	11†	11	2
Independent	*16*	......	......	......	*12*	*4*
Self-supporting	2	......	......	......	2	......
Contributing	14	......	......	......	10	4
Percentage						
Total	100.0	100.0	100.0	100.0	100.0	100.0
Dependent	*95.5*	*100.0*	*100.0*	*100.0*	*58.6*	*33.3*
Totally	88.8	100.0	100.0	84.3	20.7	....
Partially	6.7	....	....	15.7	37.9	33.3
Independent	*4.5*	....	....	....	*41.4*	*66.7*
Self-supporting	0.6	....	....	....	6.9	....
Contributing	3.9	....	....	....	34.5	66.7

* Children earning less than $12 in the year are classified as *totally dependent;* from $12 to 85 per cent of their maintenance costs, as *partially dependent;* over 85 per cent of their costs, as *independent.* Of the latter, those giving the family more than their own costs were considered *contributing.*

† Of these 11 children earning small sums at part-time employment, 3 were 11 years old, 4 were 13, 1 was 14, 3 were 15.

cent of their own costs; 2, 0.6 per cent, were self-supporting; and 14, or 3.9 per cent, not only supported themselves but also contributed to the support of their parents and brothers and sisters.[15]

[15] Children earning less than $12 in the year are classified as *totally dependent;* from $12 to 85 per cent of their maintenance costs, as *partially dependent;* over 85 per cent of their costs, as *independent.* Of the last-mentioned, those giving the family more than their own costs are classed as *contributing.*

No children under seventeen were independent; none under eleven earned anything. Girls were a greater financial liability than boys; of children under fifteen, the boys were more likely to get part-time jobs than were the girls, and once past the legal working age, fewer boys than girls remained totally dependent.

Sixteen is the legal minimum working age in California except in special circumstances. Only eleven, or 3 per cent, of the 323 children under sixteen earned anything. Of the thirty-five childrne sixteen and older, less than half were actually self-supporting. Six of the thirty-five earned nothing and were totally dependent upon their parents. Fourteen were contributing more than their own costs to the family purse.

Contributions of relatives.—In fifteen families a relative was living in the household who paid to the family at least part of the costs of his board and lodging, and often contributed additional sums to the family support. The contributions of such relatives averaged $20 a month ($245.30 per year mean, $240 median), but varied from $22.50 to $779 for the year, the latter sum from two brothers-in-law.

Eight families received money from relatives elsewhere, but in only one case was the money reported to have come from Mexico. In five cases the sum was less than $100 for the year. In no case were large sums sent to cover periods of unemployment or illness, but rather as gifts from more well-to-do relatives.

Other income.—Other sources of income, such as boarders and lodgers, rentals from property, insurance payments, a pension, sale of an automobile or of personal property, were reported by only a few families, and although an occasional family might receive a large sum from one of these sources, such cases were too rare to be of importance to the group as a whole. The average family of the 100 studied received less than 1 per cent of its total income from any of the sources named.

Income in kind.—Only ten families reported receiving no income in kind. The difficulties of evaluation already noted make it impossible to say what proportion of the total income was received in this form, but in many families it is obvious that the cash income was not a completely adequate representation of the goods and services enjoyed during the year. Sixty families reported additions to cash income in the form of food grown in their gardens, milk at reduced rates, slightly wilted and discarded vegetables and fruit from the markets, gifts of food from friends and relatives. Forty-six families received clothing, usually second-hand garments. Forty-seven gathered wood along the tracks or the beach or received it from yards and shops where they worked. The greatest assistance came in times of illness, the nightmare of low-income groups. Almost all these families were eligible for free or part-pay medical care at the hospitals and clinics, and sixty-three availed themselves of this service. Only five of the 100 families paid for hospital care in full, one paid part of the expense, and nineteen received completely free hospital care. Many other miscellaneous gifts were reported by a few families, but none of importance to the group as a whole.

Income per consumption unit.—In comparing the economic status of two Mexican families or of the average Mexican family with families in another study it is not sufficient to base a judgment of relative financial well-being on the size of the income alone. Allowance must be made for differences in size and composition of the family. Other conditions being equal, a couple with $100 a month and one or two young children is obviously better off than a larger family with older children and the same income.

Periodic attempts have been made in cost of living studies to relate income to size of family. The procedure has usually been to translate the household into equivalent adult male units. Thus a comparison of the incomes of two dissimilar families may be made in terms of dollars per adult male. Among the earliest of such scales was the "quet" of Ernst Engel, which was a consumption unit, though not in terms of the adult male. By this scale the expense of an infant at birth was fixed as 100 and ten units were added for each subsequent year until maturity.[16]

---

[16] Engel, Ernst, *Cost of production of human beings* (1883). See Williams, Faith M., "Scales for family measurement," *Proceedings of the American Statistical Association* (March 1930): 135–139.

The most significant attempt at a complete consumption unit scale in this country was made by Sydenstricker and King in an investigation of the budgets of South Carolina cotton mill families in 1917.[17] This was a scale of "ammains" and "fammains," derived from the reports of expenditures of the cotton mill families. The ammain is a unit representing a "gross demand for articles of consumption having a total money value equal to that demanded by the average male in that class at the age when his total requirements for expense of maintenance reach a maximum." The fammain is the unit of a scale of food costs relative to the cost for an adult male. This scale was compiled by adjusting the Atwater scale of caloric requirements by age and sex to fit the actual expenditures of families of specified composition. In computing the scale for articles other than food only those expenditures were included which could be charged directly to one or another member of the family. This latter scale was combined with the food scale, fammains, to arrive at the ammain.

E. L. Kirkpatrick has been actively engaged for the past few years in experiments with an elaborate series of cost consumption units for expenditure studies of farm families.[18] In Kirkpatrick's system each subdivision of expenditure—food, rent, clothing, etc.— has its own scale of relative costs for different ages and sexes, derived from the study in hand. The final scale takes account of the number of persons in the family and the greater possibility of economies in larger families, as well as differences in age and sex. The total expenditure for each item is divided by the number of cost consumption units in the family for that item, and the sum of these quotients gives the total expenditure per cost consumption unit. There is no single index of the number of equivalent adult males in the family as in the "ammain" and similar scales.

---

[17] Sydenstricker, Edgar, and King, Willford I., "The measurement of the relative economic status of families," *Quarterly Publications of the American Statistical Association*, XVII (1921): 842–857.

[18] See especially "The standard of life in a typical section of diversified farming," Cornell University Agricultural Experiment Station, *Bulletin* 423 (1923); and "Comparison of two scales for measuring the cost or value of family living," *American Journal of Sociology*, XXXVII (1931): 424–434.

Other authors are willing to use a scale of relative food requirements for different ages and sexes to compute the relative costs for other items and the total family expenditure per equivalent adult male, on the assumption that there is a high correlation between relative food requirements, food costs, and costs for other items according to age and sex.[19]

It seemed inadvisable to adopt any of these scales for use in the present study. Cost consumption units like those of Sydenstricker and King, and Kirkpatrick, which were based on the data gathered from a specific group of families, may be wholly inapplicable to another social group at a later date. The relative cost of children and adults may be greatly changed by differences in standards of living, a higher minimum working age, the increased use of special and more expensive diets for young children, the development of new wants, a change in relative price levels. There is no adequate ground for assuming that the relationship between the costs of a man and a young child which was true for South Carolina mill families in 1917 or for New York farm families in 1922 would hold good for Mexican workingmen's families in California in 1930. The use of a scale designed to measure relative caloric requirements as an indication of relative costs of quite other items appeared indefensible.

In this study, as in others, it was desirable to adopt some method by which families of different sizes could be compared and which would furnish a rough measure of economic well-being regardless of the size of family. No general scale of consumption units was set up which could be applied to all families, because it was felt that 100 families were not an adequate sample on which to base such a scale. Instead, each family was treated separately.

The expenditure per consumption unit in each family was computed by combining the food expenditure per equivalent adult male and the per capita expenditures for all other items. The scale of cost consumption units which was used in measuring food expendi-

---

[19] Zimmerman, Carle C., and Black, John D., "How Minnesota farm family incomes are spent," University of Minnesota Agricultural Experiment Station, *Bulletin* 234 (1927). See also Kirkpatrick, "Comparison of two scales."

tures is based on the relative costs of a minimum standard diet for adults and children.[20] The total annual expenditure for food was divided by the number of cquivalent adult males fed during the year according to this scale, making allowance for absences. Thus the cost of food per equivalent adult male was obtained.

Expenditures for each of the other categories, such as rent and clothing, were divided by the number of persons in the household whose expenses for this item were paid from general family funds, again making allowance for absences. The sum of the expenditures per capita for items other than food was then added to the expenditure for food per equivalent adult male, giving the total family expenditure per consumption unit. In order to get the number of consumption units per family, the total family expenditure was then divided by the expenditure per consumption unit.[21]

This procedure is not so desirable as a generalized scale suitable to this group would be, because it does not allow for age and sex differences in the cost of items other than food. The available data, however, were inadequate for the computation of such a scale.

---

[20] See below, p. 33.

[21] Example 1.

A household of five persons—man, wife, and three dependent children under sixteen. All members of the household were at home throughout the year.

$ 456.00 total expenditure for food ÷ 4.7 equivalent adult
              male units..$ 97.02 per E.A.M.
   599.85 all other items ÷ 5... 119.97 per capita
              $180.00 housing
                23.05 house operation
                31.80 furnishings
               167.85 clothing
               197.15 other
$1055.85 total family expenditure

       Total expenditure per unit.............................$216.99
       $1055.85 ÷ $216.99..................4.9 consumption units

Example 2.

A household of twelve persons—man, wife, nine children, the eldest twenty, the youngest born two months before the close of the year, and the wife of the eldest son, who lived with the family for twenty-two weeks. Other members of the family were at home throughout the year. The eldest son gave the family half his wages, for which he and his wife received food and shelter and the items incidental thereto which appear under "house operation" and "furnishings," and paid their other expenses from his own funds. The second son paid for his own clothes and amusements. These three were charged only

This procedure is more satisfactory than a simple statement of income per capita, because (1) it makes allowance for age and sex differences in the costs of food, the most important single item of the family budget and the item most considerably affected by such differences; (2) it takes account of absences from home for part of the year; (3) it makes allowance for the presence of persons like lodgers, independent relatives, or grown children, who contributed only a part of their income to the general family funds and received only a part of their support, usually board and lodging, from these funds.

The average family in this study consisted of about five consumption units (5.2 mean, 4.9 median), and reported a total expenditure between $250 and $300 per unit per year ($290.18 mean, $265.44 median). Like the total income per family, these sums showed great variation, ranging from $80 per unit per year to $726 per unit.

There appears to be a distinct negative relationship between the number of cost consumption units in the family and the expenditure per consumption unit; in other words, the larger the family the smaller the available expenditure per member. To some extent this may reflect a flaw in the cost consumption scale used, showing that too great weight was given to children relative to adults and that no allowance was made for the possibility of economies in larger families. Since, however, 80 per cent of the average family's income was derived from the father's earnings, and since the men

---

with their share of the family expenditure for food, housing, house operation, and furnishings—in the case of the girl, for twenty-two weeks only. The youngest child was charged with a share in the family expenses for only ten weeks.

$ 766.50 total expenditure for food ÷ 9.8 equivalent
           adult male units.. $78.21 per E.A.M.
    454.93 ÷ (10+1×10 weeks÷52+1×22 weeks÷52).... 42.88 per capita
        $270.00 housing
        170.48 house operation
        14.45 furnishings
    521.75 all other items÷(8+1×10 weeks÷52).............. 63.71 per capita

$1743.18 total family expenditure

        Total expenditure per unit..............................$184.80
        $1743.18÷$184.80..............9.4 consumption units

were of a class whose maximum earning power comes early in life, there was obviously but little tendency for the total income to increase with the size of the family. Accordingly, the smaller expenditure—that is to say, income—per unit in the large families represents, to some extent, greater poverty.

TABLE 11

TOTAL ANNUAL EXPENDITURE PER CONSUMPTION UNIT

Total annual expenditure per consumption unit	Number of families	Percentage of all families
All amounts	100	....
Not available	7	....
Total reported	93	100.0
$75.00–$124.99	3	3.2
125.00– 174.99	10	10.7
175.00– 224.99	17	18.3
225.00– 274.99	19	20.4
275.00– 324.99	20	21.5
325.00– 374.99	8	8.6
375.00– 424.99	4	4.3
425.00– 474.99	4	4.3
475.00– 524.99	1	1.1
525.00– 574.99	1	1.1
575.00– 624.99	4	4.3
625.00– 674.99	....	......
675.00– 724.99	1	1.1
725.00– 774.99	1	1.1

Average	
Mean	$290.18
Median	265.44

Surpluses and deficits.—Forty-three of the 100 families reported that they broke even for the year. Nine had small sums of money—all less than $25—on hand;[22] two refused to say whether they had a surplus or deficit at the close of the year. Forty-six, one of whom refused to tell the amount, reported that expenditures had exceeded

---

[22] Unlike the usage in certain other studies, money saved or invested during the year is classified among expenditures.

income. These deficits included unpaid bills, usually to the grocery store, money borrowed, and money drawn from savings. Most of the deficits took the form of unpaid bills, which usually amounted to less than $100. Thirty-six families reported unpaid bills, of which all but three were less than $100, and the majority less than $50. Nine families drew on previous years' savings, six of them for sums less than $100. The family that drew out $300 to make the last

TABLE 12

SURPLUSES AND DEFICITS REPORTED AT CLOSE OF YEAR

Surplus or deficit at close of year	Number reporting	Average amount	
		Mean	Median
Money on hand............................	9	$ 14.22	$ 15.00
Income and expenditures equal...	43	....	....
No report......................................	2	....	....
Deficit..	46*	81.75	45.00
Unpaid bills.............................	36†	40.31	30.00
Borrowed.................................	10†	95.00	100.00
Drawn from savings...............	9	143.89	75.00
Not allocated..........................	2‡	59.00	59.00

* Includes one family which reported a deficit but refused to report the amount; it is therefore not included in the averages.

† Includes one family which reported a $65 deficit covering both bills and borrowings, without indicating the amount of each; the deficit is therefore not included in the averages.

‡ Includes (both in averages and in number reporting) the family mentioned in the preceding footnote.

payment on a house they were purchasing, cannot be considered to have had a true deficit. The family already mentioned, where the man had only five weeks' work in the year, drew out $550 for living expenses. Ten families borrowed money, five less than $100, five between $100 and $200. For the forty-five families reporting deficits the median amount was $45.

Unexplained discrepancies between income and expenditure.—The standard of reliability chosen for the study was that no schedule should be included which showed an unexplained discrepancy between income and expenditure greater than 10 per cent of the income.[23] Without exact household accounts it is, of course, impossible to report with accuracy every expenditure. On the other hand, in an expense estimate the total of which varies greatly from the family's total resources, the accuracy of any of the component detail is doubtful.

In forty-seven families the estimated expenses were less than the reported income after allowance had been made for actual surpluses and deficits; in fifty-three they were more, and in the latter cases the difference tended to be greater. However, of the 100 families, seventy-eight reported discrepancies smaller than 5 per cent of income, and the average was only 3 per cent (3.4 per cent mean, 2.6 per cent median). The average total expenditure exceeded the average total income by $45.33 mean, $75.47 median.

---

[23] One exception was made, a family where income, as defined on page 14, amounted to only $156, supplemented by $550 drawn from savings. The unexplained discrepancy of $32 was 20 per cent of $156, but less than 5 per cent of the total known cash receipts.

IV

EXPENDITURE

Distribution of expenditures.—Food is the chief item in any low-income budget. Among these Mexican families it accounted for more than one-third of the total expenditure[24] (36.6 per cent mean, 35.7 per cent median), or about $500 a year. Housing cost 16 per cent, or slightly over $200; clothing about 13 per cent, or about $175. The costs of house operation—fuel, cleaning supplies, laundry, etc.—amounted to about 5 per cent, or $75. These four major items were a part of the budget of every family, except two families which lived in the section house, rent-free throughout the year. Every family reported expenditures for care of the person, a category which included barber and hairdresser and personal cleaning supplies. This was, however, a small item amounting to 2 per cent of the total, or about $30. All but two families reported expenditures for transportation—carfare and railway fares. Travel expenses greatly increased transportation costs for a few families, but the majority spent less than 25 cents a week, a small fraction of the total expenditure. Automobiles were a disproportionate expense for the twenty-six families which owned them, costing an average of $150 a year. All but one family reported some of the recreational costs grouped as leisure-time activities. The average expenditure for this group of items was about 5 or 6 per cent of the total, or between $75 and $100 a year. Three-fourths or more of the families also reported expenditures for furnishings, insurance and savings, medical care, and charity, the last-named category including gifts to church, to charitable agencies, and to dependents outside the household. Of these, only investments amounted on the average to more than $50 a year. Forty-two families spent small amounts for association dues, and twenty-eight for educational expenses.

---

[24] All such percentages are calculated on the basis of the total expenditure, not the total income, but the two were practically synonymous. (See preceding page.)

Incidental and various miscellaneous expenses in sixty-three families were lumped together in a single category of "other expenses." For the average family, even in this low-income group, the so-called basic necessaries—food, clothing, the house and its upkeep—took only 70 per cent of the total budget, leaving 30 per cent for

TABLE 13

AMOUNT AND PERCENTAGE OF ANNUAL EXPENDITURE FOR THE MAIN ITEMS OF THE FAMILY BUDGET*

Item	Number reporting	Average annual expenditure for families reporting			
		Mean		Median	
		Amount	Percentage	Amount	Percentage
Total expenditure	100	$1382.68	100.0	$1349.22	100.0
Food	100	506.58	36.6	481.65	35.7
Clothing	100	188.50	13.6	172.71	12.8
Housing	98	225.57	16.2	216.00	15.9
House operation	100	78.74	5.7	69.58	5.2
Furniture and furnishings	89	40.92	3.0	27.90	2.1
Care of the person	100	34.41	2.5	29.60	2.2
Leisure time	99	90.44	6.5	71.00	5.3
Automobile	26	158.68	10.5	142.50	10.1
Other transportation	98	26.31	1.9	12.00	0.9
Investments	80	83.51	5.7	52.20	3.7
Medical care	73	39.06	2.8	30.00	2.3
Associations	42	8.51	0.6	9.00	0.6
Education	28	29.79	1.9	18.00	1.1
Charity	85	16.83	1.2	10.00	0.7
Other	63	61.65	4.3	25.00	1.8

* See also Appendix B.

secondary expenses, of which the most important were leisure-time activities, insurance and savings, and an automobile for those families which owned one.

Food.—The average expenditure for food was about $500 per year per family ($506.58 mean, $481.65 median). Reported expenditures ranged from $242 to $1048, but seldom exceeded $700. Most of this money was spent for food materials to be prepared at home. Thirty-eight families reported costs for meals in restaurants averaging between $30 and $40 a year, usually the husband's or school children's lunches. Thirty reported small miscellaneous food expenses.

Although it was impossible, without a day by day record of purchases, to report exactly the amounts and kinds of food consumed by these families, a general idea of their diet may be obtained from two sources. Eighty-seven families gave detailed estimates of their weekly food expenditure listed by the main categories of foodstuffs—bread, meat, milk, etc. In addition, fifty families reported their daily menus for the week immediately preceding the investigator's visit.

The eighty-seven families which reported details of food expenditures spent an average of $9.50 a week, approximately the average for the whole group. One-seventh was spent for meat, one-eighth for milk, one-tenth for fruit and vegetables, nearly one-half for dry groceries, one thirty-third for butter. Comparing this with the distribution of costs in three standard food allowances for a family of similar composition, it is apparent that the chief dietary errors of the Mexicans consisted in spending too little for milk, butter, fruit, and vegetables, and too much for dry groceries—a category which includes meal for tortillas, frijoles, and other characteristic Mexican dishes. The inadequacy of the butter allowance was especially marked.[25] In comparison with fifty-four laborers' families in Chicago, chiefly Negro and Polish, with slightly higher incomes, the Mexicans showed the same tendency to spend relatively little for butter, fruit, and vegetables, and large sums for dry groceries. The Chicago families, all but two of whose diets were inadequate from a nutritional point of view, spent no greater proportion for milk, and considerably more for meat; in the latter respect the Mexicans' habits more closely approached the standard distributions of food expenditure.

The Mexican immigrant to the United States clings to the diet of his own country.[26] The diet of the working classes of Mexico is

[25] Most Mexican families use margarine.
[26] Gamio, *The Mexican immigrant.*

TABLE 14

COMPARATIVE DISTRIBUTION OF AVERAGE WEEKLY FOOD EXPENDITURE IN 87
MEXICAN FAMILIES,* IN THE NESBITT STANDARD FOOD BUDGET FOR A FAMILY
OF COMPOSITION SIMILAR TO THE AVERAGE MEXICAN FAMILY,¶ IN THE OKEY
AND HUNTINGTON STANDARD BUDGET FOR A SIMILAR FAMILY,§ IN THE STAND-
ARD SUGGESTED BY SHERMAN,† AND IN 54 CHICAGO LABORERS' FAMILIES‡

Item	87 Mexican families		Nesbitt standard budget for family similar to Mexican average	Okey and Huntington standard budget for similar family	Sherman suggested standard	54 Chicago laborers' families
	Mean expenditure per family	Percentage of total weekly expenditure	Percentage of total weekly expenditure			
Total per week	$9.50	100	100	100	100	100
Meat, fish, poultry	1.41	15	13	11	} 20 or less }	} 32
Eggs	.73	8	3	4		
Milk	1.13	12	20	17	20 or more	11
Fruit and vegetables	.94	10	20	26	20 or more	19
Bread, cakes, etc.	.66	7	10	12	}	13
Butter	.30	3	17	9		8***
Dry groceries	4.21	44	17	21	} 40** }	} 17
Candy and ice cream	.10	1	....	....		
Other	.02	....	....	....		

* The other 13 families failed to report details of food expenditure.
¶ Nesbitt, Florence, "Study of a minimum standard of living for dependent families in Los
Angeles," Community Welfare Federation, Los Angeles, *Bulletin* No. 1 (November 1927).
§ Okey, Ruth, and Huntington, Emily H., "Adequate food at low cost," *Pacific Coast Journal
of Nursing*, XXVIII (1932): 279-283.
† Sherman, H. C., *Chemistry of food and nutrition* (1926): 559.
‡ Houghteling, Leila, *The income and standard of living of unskilled laborers in Chicago* (1927),
Appendix D.
** Twenty per cent to cereals, part of which are included under "dry groceries," 20 per cent
to all other items.
*** Includes other fats.

practically limited to maize and beans, prepared with fats and
sauces in a variety of dishes, coffee to drink, and meat when
finances permit.[27] The menus reported by fifty families confirm the
persistence of native food habits. Of the fifty families, 95 per cent
served tortillas regularly, twice a day in the average family, which

[27] Thompson, Wallace, *The people of Mexico* (1921): 257-286. Redfield,
Robert, *Tepoztlan, a Mexican village* (1930): 39-41.

explains the scarcity of bread and butter shown in table 14. Some women still ground the corn in their own metates, some used commercial meal. The other Mexican staple, beans, was served every day in 72 per cent of the households reporting, and on alternate days in 20 per cent more. Coffee was the chief drink; only ten families reported serving tea at any meal; chocolate was equally rare; milk was seldom served to adults. The average family had meat once a day. Potatoes, rice, and pastes were not popular. In the average family potatoes appeared at about three meals a week, rice and pastes less often than one meal every third day. The most serious deficiency in these diets, as already noted, was a shortage of dairy products, fruit, and vegetables. The menus showed that thirty-eight of the fifty families served no fruit at meals, and five no salad nor vegetables other than potatoes. Only twenty of the fifty families served a vegetable as often as once a day. Equally strange to Americans, but of little dietary importance, is the fact that forty-two of the fifty families never served a dessert of any sort.

The Mexican peon who retained the food habits of his native country would consider himself well fed at the table of the average family studied. It has been asserted that the typical Mexican diet of maize, beans, and fats provides adequate nutritive values in assimilable form for a man engaged in heavy labor, though not for women and children.[28] Obviously, however, it does not provide the milk and butter, fresh fruits and vegetables demanded by accepted modern standards of nutrition, particularly for growing children. The usual argument in such circumstances, that Mexicans are accustomed to poorer food and lower standards of living than North Americans and Europeans, is well answered by Florence Nesbitt:

The greatest care should be used in ascribing to nationality or race any difference in necessary cost of maintaining a minimum normal standard of living. Insofar as this standard is limited to necessities for health there can be no difference based upon these conditions.

A family in one of our recent immigration groups may be content with a standard which does not furnish the minimum necessities, but the effect of

---

[28] Thompson, *op. cit.*, 280–285.

under-feeding and bad living conditions is just as disastrous to their children as it would be to an American family.[29]

She quotes in proof the infant mortality statistics for Los Angeles (1923) showing the infant death rate of Mexicans to be three times that of the white population.[30] It may be noted in this connection that the outdoor relief budget for the Los Angeles County charities adopted in February 1928, which is also used in San Diego, reduces the standard food budget 20 per cent for Mexican families.[31]

Since no attempt was made to study actual food intake of these families, the adequacy of their diet can be quantitatively measured only in terms of how far their expenditures for food were adequate to meet the cost of a standard ration, which in this instance is the series of diets for persons of different sexes and ages compiled by Florence Nesbitt in Los Angeles in 1927 for the use of the local charities[32] with prices adjusted for the lapse of time. The cost for each person's ration in the Nesbitt budget was computed in terms of the cost for a man at moderate work, or as "equivalent adult male units." Each Mexican household was then translated into terms of these units, making deductions for absences and for meals eaten away from home. The expenditure for food per unit was then computed and compared with the adjusted Nesbitt standard to determine how far each family fell short of the money expenditure necessary to purchase a ration adequate and balanced according to this standard.[33]

---

[29] "Study of a minimum standard of living for dependent families in Los Angeles," *The Community Welfare Federation, Los Angeles, Bulletin No. 1* (November 1927): 34.

Of course it may be urged that Mexicans get their food more cheaply than was contemplated by this standard diet—as is discussed below—but in view of the general prejudice which tends to drive Mexican allowances far below the level of other national groups, it seems important to preserve the general standard.

[30] In San Diego in 1928 the infant mortality rate was 48 for the city as a whole, 102 for the Mexicans. San Diego County Health Department (letter, December 2, 1931).

[31] San Francisco furnishes a special diet for Mexicans; Alameda County makes no distinction.

[32] *Op. cit.*

[33] Gifts of food and purchases of slightly stale foodstuffs at reduced price will, of course, lower the money expenditure necessary to secure adequate food. See below.

The adjusted Nesbitt allowance for a man at moderate work was $140.92 a year, or 39 cents a day. The average Mexican household in this study—4.5 equivalent adult male units—spent slightly over $100 a year per man ($113.17 mean, $102.78 median), or between

TABLE 15

Expenditure for Food per Equivalent Adult Male Unit

Annual expenditure for food per e.a.m. unit		Number of families	Percentage of 93 families
All families		100	....
Information not available		7	....
Total reported		93	100.0
Percentage of standard allowance	Amount spent		
30.0– 39.9	$42.28–$56.36	3	3.2
40.0– 49.9	56.37– 70.45	8	8.6
50.0– 59.9	70.46– 84.54	10	10.7
60.0– 69.9	84.55– 98.63	17	18.3
70.0– 79.9	98.64–112.73	13	14.0
80.0– 89.9	112.74–126.82	11	11.8
90.0– 99.9	126.83–140.91	9	9.7
– – – – – – – – – – – – – standard – – – – – – – – – – –			
100.0–109.9	140.92–155.00	9	9.7
110.0–119.9	155.01–169.09	6	6.4
120.0–129.9	169.10–183.19	1	1.1
130.0–139.9	183.20–197.28	4	4.3
140.0–149.9	197.29–211.37	....	....
150.0–159.9	211.38–255.46	2	2.2
Average			
Mean	80.3 per cent	$113.17	
Median	72.9 per cent	102.78	

20 and 25 per cent below standard. The amounts spent per man varied from $50 to $217, or from a 64 per cent deficit to a 53 per cent surplus. Forty-four per cent of the families spent between $85 and $127, that is, from 60 to 90 per cent of the requirement. Eleven families reported deficiencies greater than 50 per cent. The expen-

ditures of sixty-two families were at least 10 per cent below standard, and those of fifty-one families were more than 20 per cent below. Twenty-two families reported spending more than the standard.

The fifty-one families with a serious deficiency in their food expenditures were, on the whole, the larger and poorer families of the group. The average family of the fifty-one whose expenditure for food was 20 per cent or more below standard had one or two more mouths to feed and one-third less total expenditure per consumption unit than the average for the families whose food expenditure was approximately standard or above.

It is obvious that undernourishment, according to accepted dietetic standards, was prevalent in this group of Mexican families, so far as the amount spent for food is an index of the nutritive value of the diet. Certainly two-thirds of the families spent too little to purchase an adequate food supply, and probably their numbers were augmented by others who spent enough to buy the standard allowance, but did not spend it intelligently.

It must be borne in mind that the amount spent for food does not represent all the food consumed in every household. Some families bought slightly wilted fruits and vegetables or stale bread at greatly reduced prices. Others, living on the waterfront, were given fish from the boats. In other cases, deficiencies in food purchased were modified to some extent by the additional food supplies from gardens, chickens, and goats, from vegetables and fruit discarded at the markets or donated by friends and relatives, and from leftovers from restaurants or stores where the man worked. Sixty families reported such additions to their purchased food, but in at least nineteen of these cases the amount was insignificant, worth $15 or less. In most cases it was very difficult to determine the extent of supplementary food, since neither the quantity nor the value was reported. On careful examination of the schedules, it seemed improbable that this extra food ever equalled the amount of the deficit. Of the families which spent less than 80 per cent of the standard allowance, not half received appreciable supplements in food.

Clothing.—The average family spent about $175 a year ($188.50 mean, $172.71 median), or 13 per cent of its total budget, on clothing for its five or six members. Three families of four, five, and eight members respectively, all with annual incomes less than $525, spent less than $50 on clothes for the whole family. The three largest expenditures were between $400 and $500, all in families with incomes of $1800 to $2100.

TABLE 16

Number of Families Reporting a Specified Expenditure
for Clothing, and the Number of Such Families Which
Received Gifts of Clothing Within the Year

Annual expenditure	Number of families spending specified amount for clothing	Number of families receiving gifts of clothing
All amounts................................	100	45
Less than $50.00............................	3	3
$50.00–$99.99................................	14	7
100.00–149.99................................	24	13
150.00–199.99................................	19	9
200.00–249.99................................	16	3
250.00–299.99................................	10	4
300.00–349.99................................	8	3
350.00–399.99................................	3	1
400.00–449.99................................	2	1
450.00–499.99................................	1	1

Average

Mean..	$188.50
Median..	172.71

About the same amount of the total clothing expenditure, approximately $50, was apportioned to husband and to wife (man: $52.54 mean, $44 median; woman: $51.49 mean, $43.50 median), and about half as much, on the average, to each child in the family (average per child: $25.31 mean, $21.67 median).

The cost of the husband's clothing ranged from $2.90 to $184.50. All but one of the expenditures were less than $120; half were between $25 and $75.

The cost of the wife's clothing covered almost the same range, the highest expenditure being $175.60. Fifty-two per cent of the women spent between $20 and $60; 18 per cent spent less than $20. The average clothing expenditure for employed women was approximately the same as for the housewives. Of the ten women who spent $100 to $175, however, six were employed.

The average expenditure per child for clothing ranged from $1.73 to $69.40 per year. In 60 per cent of the cases the expenditure was between $10 and $30. These figures, like all the expenditures reported in this study, are limited to those items paid from the family purse. Older children who were working and bought their own clothes may have spent more. There was no marked relationship between the number of children in the family and the clothing expenditure per child.

The Mexican immigrant may cling to his native food-habits, but he rapidly adopts American dress. The clothing purchases reported were overalls, wool suits, ready-made dresses, silk stockings, corsets, felt hats, instead of the native muslin trousers and blouse, calico dress, straw hat, and reboso of Mexico. The tables in Appendix A attempt to depict the wardrobe and annual clothing purchases of certain typical persons in the group studied.

The average man bought a $26 suit every four years and a $3.50 hat every two years. He owned no overcoat. His everyday working costume was overalls or separate pants and $1 shirts. He wore neckties only for dress. He did not buy nightclothes. The woman of the family habitually wore cotton house dresses at $1, but she owned two "best" dresses, costing $9 each, two cheap hats, and silk stockings for street wear. A boy of twelve or older, whose clothes were bought by his family, had a new suit every two years. Like his father, his usual costume was a cheap cotton shirt with overalls or pants, cap, and sweater. Girls under twelve wore cotton dresses costing 75 cents apiece, and owned a better dress at $2, which was replaced every second year. Hats, bought every third year, were obviously worn only on special occasions. They wore socks instead of stockings.

Housing costs.—The items included under this category are rent, or interest and installments paid on a house, taxes and assessments, fire insurance, repairs, water, plants and fertilizer for the garden, and garage rent. Families which were renting very seldom paid for any of the other items; water costs were included in the rent seven times out of eight, and only five tenant families reported expenditures for garden or repairs; their housing expenditures may be taken as practically synonymous with rent. Two families lived the whole year, one for ten and one-half months, and one for one month, in the section houses.[34] Eighty-five families (including for certain months the last two mentioned) paid rent; thirteen owned their homes,[35] but nine of these were still paying on the mortgage. No family in this group began to purchase a house in the year of this study.

The owners did not differ appreciably from other families of the group as regards occupation, expenditure per consumption unit, or size of family, but the men were older. None were under thirty, and the average age was thirty-five.

The eighty-four families which rented their living quarters[36] paid on the average about $200 a year ($212.73 mean, $216 median). The most common rentals were $15 and $20 a month;[37] one family spent $30 and another $35. More than half spent between $150 and $250 a year.

---

[34] Maintained by the railroad for trackmen and similar employees. These were one-story buildings with six apartments, one bathroom and one outside toilet, where the railroad workers with families received as part of their wages a two-room, unheated apartment, electricity, and stove wood for cooking.

[35] It is customary in such studies to classify homes mortgaged or being bought on installments as "owned."

[36] Omitting one family which paid rent only for a month and a half, amounting to but $9. This is a much higher proportion of tenancy than was reported by the 1930 census for San Diego as a whole—52 per cent.

[37] The San Diego Realty Board reported $20 a month as the average rental of a workingman's home, $15 to $20 for the Mexican district. The Census of 1930 reported $19 as the median rental for "other races"—of which Mexicans constituted 82 per cent—in San Diego.

TABLE 17
EXPENDITURE FOR HOUSING ACCORDING TO CONDITIONS OF TENURE

Annual expenditure	Number of families spending a specified amount for housing				
	All families	Tenants	Owners		
			All owners	Owned clear	Mortgaged
			Number		
Total	100	87	13	4	9
Free housing*	3	3	....	....	....
All amounts	97	84	13	4	9
Less than $50.00	1	....	1	1	....
$50.00–$99.99	2	....	2	2	....
100.00–149.99	15	15	....	....	....
150.00–199.99	24	23	1	....	1
200.00–249.99	28	26	2	1	1
250.00–299.99	10	10	....	....	....
300.00–349.99	8	8	....	....	....
350.00–399.99	3	1	2	....	2
400.00–449.99	3	1	2	....	2
450.00–499.99	1	....	1	....	1
500.00–549.99	....	....	....	....	....
550.00–599.99	....	....	....	....	....
600.00–649.99	....	....	....	....	....
650.00–699.99	1	....	1	....	1
700.00–749.99	1	....	1	....	1
	Average†				
Mean	$227.80	$212.73	$325.21	$91.93	$428.89
Median	216.00	216.00	388.00	58.18	404.09
	Percentage				
All amounts	100.0	100.0	100.0	100.0	100.0
Less than $50.00	1.0	....	7.7	25.0	....
$50.00–$99.99	2.1	....	15.4	50.0	....
100.00–149.99	15.5	17.8	....	....	....
150.00–199.99	24.8	27.4	7.7	....	11.1
200.00–249.99	28.9	31.0	15.4	25.0	11.1
250.00–299.99	10.3	11.9	....	....	....
300.00–349.99	8.2	9.5	....	....	....
350.00–399.99	3.1	1.2	15.4	....	22.2
400.00–449.99	3.1	1.2	15.4	....	22.2
450.00–499.99	1.0	....	7.7	....	11.1
500.00–549.99	....	....	....	....	....
550.00–599.99	....	....	....	....	....
600.00–649.99	....	....	....	....	....
650.00–699.99	1.0	....	7.7	....	11.1
700.00–749.99	1.0	....	7.7	....	11.1

* Including one family which paid only $9 rent for the year.
† Excluding the family mentioned in the preceding footnote.

Of the thirteen house owners, four carried no mortgage. Their housing costs were naturally low, $65 a year or less for three who paid only very small taxes and assessments, water, and fire insurance. One spent $207, including a heavy assessment, repairs, garden, and a large water bill. The nine who were still paying for their homes had much heavier costs than those who rented, averaging more than $400 a year ($428.89 mean, $404.09 median), and ranging from $196, which included no installments on principal, to $729, of which $500 was installments, paid by that family of the group which had the largest income. All these families also paid taxes and water costs, and seven of the nine paid assessments ranging from $7 to $60. The total taxes and assessments paid by the thirteen owners ranged from $18 to $113, averaging between $50 and $60.

Water costs were usually included in the rent, but eleven tenants in addition to the thirteen owners paid for their own water. The monthly water bills were never less than $1 and usually between $1 and $1.50.

Housing conditions.—Separate cottages were more common than flats.[38] Sixty-one families lived in detached, one-family houses. In this group were found all but one of the owners. Thirty-six were in multiple dwellings, including three which were living in section houses at the time of the investigation and one owner who rented the upper story of his house. Two families lived behind their shops. One failed to report.

Overcrowding was common. The dwellings contained from two to seven rooms, but two-thirds consisted of three or four rooms. For an average household of six persons, the average house had four rooms, or 0.6 rooms per person. Government studies set a standard of one room per person.[39] Seventy-six families, or 80 per cent of those reporting, were below standard, that is, had less than one room per person. The larger the family the more markedly was it

[38] According to the Census of 1930, 96 per cent of all dwellings in San Diego were one-family dwellings.

[39] United States Bureau of Labor Statistics, *Minimum quantity budget necessary to maintain a worker's family of five at a level of health and decency* (1920): 13.

TABLE 18

NUMBER OF ROOMS CLASSIFIED BY SIZE OF HOUSEHOLD

Number of rooms occupied	All families	Number of families occupying specified number of rooms — Size of household											
		Two	Three	Four	Five	Six	Seven	Eight	Nine	Ten	Eleven	Twelve	Thirteen
All dwellings	100	1	10	14	17	23	12	15	4	1	...	2	1
Not reported	5	...	...	...	4	...	...	1	...	...	...	...	...
Total reported	95	1	10	14	13	23	12	14	4	1	...	2	1
Two	8	1	2	3	...	1	...	1	...	...	...	...	...
Three	31	...	5	3	8	5	5	2	3	...	...	...	...
Four	33	...	3	4	4	12	4	6	...	...	...	...	...
Five	15	...	...	3	1	4	3	3	...	...	...	...	...
Six	6	...	...	1	...	1	...	2	1	...	...	1	1
Seven	2	...	...	...	...	...	...	...	...	1	...	1	...
Average number of rooms occupied (per household)													
Mean	3.9	2.0	3.1	3.7	3.5	4.0	3.8	4.2	3.8	7.0	...	6.5	5.0
Median	3.8	2.0	3.1	3.8	3.3	4.0	3.8	4.2	3.2	7.0	...	6.5	5.0
Average number of rooms per person													
Mean	0.6	1.0	1.0	0.9	0.7	0.7	0.5	0.5	0.4	0.7	...	0.5	0.4
Median	0.6	1.0	1.0	1.0	0.7	0.7	0.5	0.5	0.4	0.7	...	0.5	0.4

deficient in house room. The worst examples of overcrowding were families of six, eight, and nine persons living in two or three rooms. There was no crowding comparable to tenement conditions; only five families reported as many as three or four persons per room.

The conditions in regard to sleeping arrangements were somewhat better. Forty-three families had at least the equivalent of one single bed per person, and the average for the group was 0.9 beds per person. One household of eight reported beds for only two persons, and one of thirteen, beds for only seven. There were other marked inadequacies. Investigators reported that in most cases pallets on the floor were used instead of beds, since in Mexico the Mexican habitually sleeps rolled up in a blanket on a mat. For this reason it is difficult to judge the adequacy of their sleeping arrangements by American standards.

Sanitary equipment was notably satisfactory. Every house had running water. Seventy-eight per cent of the eighty-eight families which answered this question reported bathrooms. These were private baths in 60 per cent of the cases, and shared, usually with only one other family, in 18 per cent. Nineteen families, or 22 per cent of those reporting, had no bathroom. Families living in separate houses enjoyed markedly better conditions in this respect than families in flats or apartments. Eighty per cent of the former had private baths, and 18 per cent had none; one family shared its bathroom with another family. In multiple dwellings, 23 per cent of the families had a private bath, 27 per cent had none, and 50 per cent shared a bathroom. Only two of the thirteen owned homes had no bathroom. All but two families had water-closets—indoors and private in fifty-two cases. Fourteen private toilets were reported on back-porches or in yards; twenty-eight toilets were shared with neighbors, usually with only one other family. Four families failed to report. In four cases five or six families used the same toilet. These and two privies were apparently the only serious instances of lack of sanitary conveniences. Privies are allowed in San Diego only in such parts of the city as do not have sewer connections.

In addition to adequate sanitary provisions, the majority of houses were supplied with electricity and gas, especially if they were rented flats instead of small owned homes. Ninety were lighted by electricity, ten by oil lamps. Sixty-one were fitted with gas plates or stoves for cooking, frequently with a wood or oil stove in addition. Where gas was lacking, all but three families used a wood stove in preference to oil.

Although the majority of housewives did the family laundry, only eleven had washing machines. The most common labor-saving devices were electric irons and sewing machines, reported by eighty-four and seventy-nine families respectively. Five of the sewing machines were electric. Forty-one families had both an electric iron and a sewing machine.

In one-third of the schedules the investigator made no comment on housing conditions. The other schedules contained comments so heterogeneous that it is impossible to present a general picture of housing conditions other than the facts already cited. The most frequent comments on the type of house were that it was an old dwelling converted into small flats, or a small, lightly constructed cottage. Scarcity of furniture and furnishings was often remarked. Cleanliness and neatness in housekeeping were noted more often than dirt and disorder. About equal numbers of dwellings were reported as sunny and airy or as dark and poorly ventilated. Nine houses were rear cottages. Four dwellings were reported as dilapidated, one as actually condemned, only two as having no yard space.

In summary it may be said that, according to any standard, the majority of families had inadequate space, and that half of them had too few beds. The typical family had a private bath and water-closet, electricity, gas, an electric iron and a sewing machine. To judge from the investigators' comments, not more than a half-dozen of these families lived in actual squalor. Cases in which housing conditions were not up to standard were less serious in the mild climate of San Diego, where much time is spent out-of-doors, than in a more severe climate.

House operation.—The average family spent about $75 ($78.74 mean, $69.58 median) for the costs of running a house, including electricity, gas, and other fuel, ice, telephone, cleaning supplies, laundry, service, and moving. The amounts ranged from $16 to $221, but few families spent over $125, and one-third spent between $20 and $50. The families with very low expenses usually had no gas and electricity or paid for it in the rent, gathered stove wood on

TABLE 19

EXPENDITURE FOR ITEMS OF HOUSE OPERATION

Item	Number of families reporting	Average annual expenditure for families reporting	
		Mean	Median
Total house operation	100	$78.74	$69.58
Fuel and light	98	37.19	31.30
Electricity	73*	15.87	12.00
Gas	53†	24.20	21.00
Wood	16	26.19	30.00
Coal	2	30.50	30.50
Kerosene	41	6.87	4.00
Laundry supplies	100	20.88	17.15
Laundry sent out—regular	39	33.00	26.00
—occasional	20	8.03	6.00
Telephone—regular rate full year	7	30.07	30.00
—other	22	2.56	.98
Service	8	24.00	15.00
Ice	10	9.33	6.00
Moving	20	6.38	5.00
Paint	2	7.15	7.15

* Excludes 7 families which paid costs for only part of year, 8 where costs were included in rent, and 4 which reported gas and electricity together; 8 families had no electricity at any time during the year.

† Excludes 6 families which paid costs for only part of year, 4 which reported gas and electricity together, and 1 which failed to report the cost; 36 had no gas at any time in the year.

the beach and, of course, did their own laundry. The highest expenditures characteristically included regular laundry service and larger light and fuel bills.

Fuel and light.—The largest item in house operation costs was fuel and light ($37.19 mean, $31.30 median) which included gas, electricity, coal, wood, and kerosene. The modal expenditure, one-fourth of all the cases, was between $10 and $20 a year, but seven spent over $75. The highest sum reported was $132. Families living in the section houses received light and fuel free. Those spending less than $10.80 a year—the minimum charge for electricity—either had no electricity and burned kerosene, or it was included in the rent. The minimum charge in San Diego for gas and electricity combined was $19.80 for twelve months; every family paying less than this amount was receiving free either stove wood or light, usually the former. On the other hand, practically none of the families spending more than $50 a year for light and fuel reported any free supplements. It has already been remarked that nearly half the group gathered its wood; Mexican children are trained to pick up driftwood on the beaches. The group average of $3 a month for light and fuel is evidently not the total cash value of the materials actually used. In addition, investigators report that Mexicans are exceedingly careful in not wasting gas and that not infrequently baking is done on a communal basis by groups of families.

Laundry supplies.—On the average, materials for laundry and house cleaning—soap, washing powder, cleansers, polishes, etc.— cost these families about $1.50 a month ($20.88 a year mean, $17.15 median). The estimates ranged from $5 to $79 a year, but half were between $10 and $20, and amounts over $25 were comparatively rare. Families which regularly patronized a commercial laundry spent on the average as much for cleaning supplies as did those which did all their washing at home.

Laundry sent out.—Despite their relatively low incomes and native customs,[40] more than one-third, thirty-nine, of the families reported laundry sent out regularly during at least a part of the year. The average cost was between $2 and $3 a month ($33 a year mean, $26 median). Four families spent more than $52 a year. Most families spending less than $26 a year used the laundries for a limited period or sent out a bundle only once a month.

In addition, twenty families sent out an occasional bundle of laundry, usually when the housewife was ill.

---

[40] There are few commercial laundries in Mexico, even in the larger cities. Thompson, *op. cit.*, 302, 366.

Telephones.—Telephone costs were not an important item in the typical family budget of this group. Seven families had telephones costing $24 to $39 a year; in another, half the cost was charged to a business conducted at home. Four others which paid nothing had the regular use of a telephone, and twenty-one reported tolls for telephone calls ranging from 5 cents to $12, but averaging only $1 or $2 a year.

Service.—People at this economic level do not keep servants. One saleswoman with a full-time job and a young child had a cleaning woman for two hours a month and paid $3 a week to have the child cared for in her absence, a total of $102 for the year. Seven families reported paid help in the house at the time of a confinement, costing from $1 to $22.50. Others relied on the unpaid assistance of relatives and friends during illness.

Ice and other items.—Ice was little used in these families. One household reported buying ice regularly throughout the year; nine others bought for briefer periods. Costs varied from $1 to $3 a month for the period of purchase. No electric refrigerators were reported.

Two purchases of paint for furniture complete the list of items catalogued as "house operation."

Furniture and furnishings.—The investigators frequently commented that the Mexicans' houses were but scantily furnished. Eleven families spent nothing for furniture or furnishings in the year, twenty-six others spent less than $10, and half of those who made purchases spent less than $30 ($40.92 mean, $27.90 median). The smaller sums were usually spent for pots and pans, dishes, brooms, bedding, or other minor items of household equipment. Seven families spent more than $100, the largest sum, $180. In seven cases the expenditures included small amounts for repairs. Forty-one families were buying furniture on installment, the payments averaging $50 a year ($51.72 mean, $49.50 median). The installment payments averaged 3.5 per cent of the total family expenditure; nine families were paying between 5 and 9 per cent. The families reporting installment payments did not differ from the main group in expenditure per consumption unit. Nor did their installment payments reduce their provision for insurance and savings. Certainly the majority of these Mexicans were not burdened by a load of installment payments for furniture.

TABLE 20

EXPENDITURE DURING THE YEAR FOR FURNITURE AND FURNISHINGS

Annual expenditure	Number of families spending a specified amount			
	Total	Installment payments	Other purchases	Repairs
All amounts.................	89	41	86	7
Less than $25.00..........	38	9	65	7
Less than $5.00.........	*15*	....	*23*	*6*
$5.00–$9.99...............	*11*	*3*	*18*	*1*
10.00–14.99................	*4*	....	*7*	....
15.00–19.99................	*6*	....	*11*	....
20.00–24.99................	*2*	*6*	*6*	....
$25.00–$49.99...............	20	12	14	....
50.00– 74.99................	11	12	5	....
75.00– 99.99................	13	5	2	....
100.00–124.99................	3	2	....	....
125.00–149.99................	3	....	....	....
150.00–174.99................	....	1	....	....
175.00–199.99................	1	....	....	....
Average				
Mean............................	$40.92	$51.72	$17.42	$3.36
Median..........................	27.90	49.50	11.50	3.50

Care of the person.—This category includes the costs of barber and beauty parlor and of personal cleaning supplies. The last-named classification covers the ordinary bathroom-closet drugs and medical supplies, cosmetics, soap, toothbrushes and paste, shaving cream and razor blades, and similar items.

These Mexican families did not economize by cutting the men's and children's hair at home. All but six men patronized a barber, spending most commonly 50 cents or 75 cents a month ($7.53 a year mean, $6 median). One man spent 50 cents a week. In sixty-two families the children's hair was cut by a barber, at an average cost of 60 cents a month. Twenty-three wives reported expenses for haircuts, usually 50 cents a month. Six families reported occasional marcels for some of their members and one family reported other beauty parlor expenses. The average bill for barber and beauty parlor—the latter a rare item—was $14 a year. Five families spent nothing, nine more than $25, none over $50 for the year.

TABLE 21

EXPENDITURE FOR CARE OF THE PERSON

Item	Number of families reporting	Average annual expenditure for families reporting		Average regardless of number reporting
		Mean	Median	
Total................................	100	$34.41	$29.60	$34.41
Barber—husband...........	94	7.53	6.00	7.08
—wife.....................	23	5.30	6.00	1.22
—children...........	62	7.75	7.20	4.80
Marcels, etc.....................	7	8.79	9.00	.62
Personal cleaning supplies................................	96	21.56	18.70	20.69

The typical family spent $1.50 to $1.75 a month for personal cleaning supplies ($21.56 a year mean, $18.70 median). The expenditures ranged from $1.25 to $87 for the year, but only six families spent more than $50, and 70 per cent of the families spent less than $25. Four families, all with low total expenditures per consumption unit, spent absolutely nothing for personal cleaning supplies during the year; they used laundry soap for washing and shaving, and did without cosmetics, toothbrushes, and the other small items of this nature, usually considered indispensable.

Total expenditures for care of the person—barber and personal cleaning supplies—averaged about $30 a year ($34.41 mean, $29.60 median), and ranged from $1.25 to $116.55, but exceeded $75 in only three cases.

V

EXPENDITURE (Concluded)

Leisure-time activities.—These Mexican families spent more on the various forms of relaxation and recreation grouped under the title of leisure-time activities than on any other category of expenditure, except food, clothing, and housing. Only one family was too poor to spend anything at all for amusements; several amounts were insignificant; expenditures were reported up to $365. The variation in expenditure was great, with no pronounced central tendency ($90.44 mean, $71 median), probably because of the multiplicity of items in the group. Two-thirds of the families spent less than $100. There appears to be a marked relationship between the amount of total expenditure per consumption unit and the amount spent for leisure time activities. As is usual, recreation costs proved elastic, quickly reduced in poverty, and expanded when family finances permitted.

Expenditures in this category do not represent the full recreational resources of these Mexicans. Central agencies, such as the city schools and Neighborhood House, offer entertainments, social contacts, libraries, various amusements, athletics, and in some cases vacations, so that a small money expenditure does not necessarily imply that the family was starved for recreation. The city schools through their evening classes supply many opportunities for amateur entertainments. As far as the Mexicans are concerned, the talent is almost always furnished by themselves; the events are in the nature of "folk" entertainment; therefore the cost to the Mexicans is slight.

The typical Mexican family spent approximately $80 for its recreation and other leisure-time activities. These took a wide variety of forms, but 70 per cent or more of the families patronized the movies, bought tobacco, and provided spending money for their children. More than half the families reported expenditures for commercial amusements other than movies, for newspapers, and for gifts. One-fourth reported purchases of radios, and one-fourth other musical instruments. Expenditures for vacations, social entertainment, reading matter other than newspapers, and hobbies of any sort were comparatively rare.

Eighty-two families reported expenditures for movies, in most cases between $5 and $25 a year ($18.07 mean, $15.30 median).

TABLE 22

EXPENDITURE FOR LEISURE-TIME ACTIVITIES

Item	Number of families reporting	Average annual expenditure for families reporting	
		Mean	Median
Total	99	$90.44	$71.00
Movies	82	18.07	15.30
Other commercial amusements	56	14.17	12.00
Newspapers	52	7.98	6.58
Other reading matter	36	3.15	3.00
Radio—payments	24	48.30	33.80
Other musical instruments and up-keep, including radio upkeep	23	18.59	10.00
Social entertainment	14	14.57	13.48
Vacation	12	39.33	20.00
Spending money—children	71	14.01	10.40
Chewing gum	32	3.09	2.60
Tobacco	75	21.91	19.50
Gifts	56	10.77	8.00
Stationery and stamps	81	3.20	2.00
Other items	28	10.33	5.30

One reported only 40 cents spent during the year; two spent $5 a month. Of the eighteen families which spent nothing for movies, one had free passes and in three other cases the children probably spent their own money for tickets. Of the remaining fourteen, thirteen had less than the average total expenditure per consumption unit. Obviously, as in American families, movie tickets were an essential feature of these Mexican families' spending ways except under pressure of a special need for economy.

Fifty-six families patronized other forms of commercial amusements, including theaters, pool, excursions, and sports events, but
none of these was as popular as movies. The average cost of these
items was about $12 a year ($14.17 mean, $12 median).

Only one family spent anything for athletics. Such activities are
ordinarily provided by schools and other agencies. An alternative
for commercial amusements is home recreation, including expenditures for reading matter, musical instruments, especially radios,
and social entertainment. There were not more than a half-dozen
families in the whole group which lacked not only commercial
amusements but also all these other sources of diversion. Fifty-two
families bought newspapers, at an average cost of about 50 cents a
month; in another the children paid for the paper; in nine other
families other reading matter was purchased. Thirty-six families
bought books or periodicals; few of them spent more than $3 during
the year. Forty-five families spent money on musical instruments
and their upkeep. Twenty-four were buying radios,[41] and half of
these spent $30 or less for that purpose although one spent $240;
two were paying for pianos; six bought phonographs. A cornet,
a banjo, a ukelele, three guitars, and three violins were also purchased. Other families spent small sums for sheet music or phonograph records. Fourteen families reported costs of social entertainment, averaging $14, which was for christenings and other fiestas.
Other families included the costs of guests in the food bill.

Only twelve families reported expenditures for vacations. In all
but one case this consisted of a visit to relatives or friends in California or over the border; the costs were usually below $50.

Hobbies, such as photography or pets, were rare.

In seventy-one families the children received spending money,
which usually amounted to less than $25 a year for all the children
of the family ($14.01 mean, $10.40 median), and did not usually
include the cost of movies. Nor did it include the money retained
by working children for their own use. Probably most of it was

---

[41] According to the 1930 census, 51 per cent of all families in San Diego
owned or were purchasing a radio.

spent for candy, ice cream, and chewing gum. Purchases of chewing gum out of family funds, averaging $3 a year, were reported by thirty-two families.

Seventy-five families reported expenditures for tobacco; one man received his tobacco as a gift. The average cost per family was $20 ($21.91 mean, $19.50 median). The highest amount was $65.

Expenditures for gifts and for stationery and stamps were also included in this category of expenditure. The latter was a common but minor item, averaging only $2 or $3 a year. Fifty-six families spent money for gifts either to members of the family or to other persons ($10.77 a year mean, $8 median); seventeen spent less than $5; the highest estimate was $35.

Automobile.—Probably only in the United States would one find ownership of an automobile in a group as low in the economic scale as were these Mexicans. One-fourth, twenty-six, of the Mexican families investigated owned and operated an automobile.[42] Nor were these automobile owners drawn exclusively from the families with some surplus over bare necessaries. The average total expenditure per consumption unit was no higher among car owners than in other families. The automobile apparently represents a diversion of money from more essential expenses, especially in view of the comparatively adequate public transportation facilities existing in San Diego. As example, automobile owners seemingly were economizing on food in order to buy gasoline. In only two of the twenty-six families was the expenditure for food per equivalent adult male equal to the standard; and twenty-one families, or 81 per cent, showed serious deficiencies in contrast to 45 per cent of the families which did not own cars.

Ownership of an automobile was in no sense an economy; the average automobile-owning family saved no more than $3 to $10 a year in carfare compared to families without automobiles. The

---

[42] In addition, one family owned an automobile which was not in use during the year, another a car for business purposes, a third had the use of the employer's car, and in a fourth family all the operating expenses were paid by a grown son. None of these families paid any automobile expenses during the year. Therefore, they are excluded from the group of automobile owners in the following consideration of expenses.

typical automobile among these Mexicans had been bought at second-hand for a comparatively small sum, was three to five years old at the time of this study, and cost about $10 a month for upkeep. Nine families either bought a car within the year or made payments on one previously bought. The sums paid ranged from $35 to two payments of approximately $200 each. All cars purchased in the year in which this study was made were second-hand.

TABLE 23

EXPENDITURE FOR AUTOMOBILES

Annual expenditure	Number of families spending a specified amount		
	All automobile costs	Payments on purchase price	Upkeep—cars owned during full year
All amounts	26	9	19*
Less than $50.00	3	2	....
$50.00–$99.99	7	5	8
100.00–149.99	5	....	5
150.00–199.99	3	1	2
200.00–249.99	3	1	3
250.00–299.99	2	....	1
300.00–349.99	....	....	....
350.00–399.99	3	....	....
Average			
Mean	$158.68	$93.78	$135.81
Median	142.50	76.00	128.00

* Excludes 5 cars operated less than a full year, one case where the employer paid for gas and oil, and one which covered the expenses on 2 cars.

In fact, only two of the twenty-six cars were bought new. Excluding seven cases where the cost of upkeep was for less than a year, was partly paid by an employer, or covered more than one car, the cost of upkeep for a full year ranged from $64.50 to $267—the mean, $135.81, the median, $128.

Other transportation.—Every family but two, both of which had the use of an automobile, spent something for carfare. In addition, two received free street-car passes worth $1 a week. The average

TABLE 24

Expenditure for Transportation

Annual expenditure	Number of families spending a specified amount			
	Total transportation costs*	Carfare		Travel costs other than vacations
		Automobile owners	Others	
All amounts......................	98	24†	71‡	13
Less than $25.00............	64	21	47	9
Less than $5.00..........	*13*	*4*	*10*	....
$5.00–$9.99.................	*18*	*6*	*11*	*2*
10.00–14.99.................	*21*	*9*	*16*	*4*
15.00–19.99.................	*9*	*1*	*9*	*2*
20.00–24.99.................	*3*	*1*	*1*	*1*
$25.00–$49.99.................	17	2	11	2
50.00– 74.99.................	13	1	11	....
75.00– 99.99.................	....	....	....	....
100.00–124.99.................	2	....	1	1
125.00–149.99.................	....	....	....	....
150.00–174.99.................	1	....	1	....
250.00–274.99.................	....	....	....	1
275.00–299.99.................	....	....	....	....
300.00–324.99.................	1	....	....	....

Average				
Mean..................................	$26.31	$13.50	$23.55	$41.62
Median..............................	12.00	10.20	12.80	15.00

* Includes $18.60 spent by one family for a bicycle.

† Excludes one family with a free street-car pass. One automobile-owning family spent nothing for carfare.

‡ Excludes one family with a free street-car pass and one with the use of a car.

cost of carfare for families owning automobiles was about $1 a month ($13.50 mean, $10.20 median).[43] Families which depended wholly on street-cars for transportation showed a much greater variance in expenditures, depending on whether the man and children walked or rode to work or school ($23.55 mean, $12.80

---

[43] The two families with passes and one with the use of a company car are excluded from this comparison.

median). Some of these expenditures were less than $1 for the whole year, thirteen over $50, and two over $100. Distances are not so great in San Diego as to prevent walking to and from the places of work.

Travel expenses in connection with a vacation have already been discussed under that heading. Thirteen families spent various sums —all but two less than $50—for trips to surrounding towns in search of work, or in one case back to Mexico for a funeral.

One family bought a bicycle for $15 and spent $3.60 for repairs.

Investments.—This category includes investments proper, that is, purchases of income property, life, health, and accident insurance premiums, and bank savings. It does not include installments paid on a house in which the family is living, for such a house is a durable use-good rather than a long-term investment and has therefore been classified under "housing." No attempt was made to ascertain the family's total holdings in the form of bank savings or income property, because of the antagonism such questions would arouse. The amount laid by during the current year has been used as sufficiently indicative of the financial status, since it is improbable that any of these families owned sufficient property to render current savings unnecessary.

Of the 100 families, eighty reported an expenditure for some form of investment, but in three cases it was merely small sums put aside in the children's school savings. The amounts reported ranged from $5 to $427 for the year. The average was less than $100 ($83.51 mean, $52.20 median). Two-thirds reported less than $75.

Obviously, therefore, about one family in four of these Mexicans could make no provision during the year for sickness, old age, or death; and certainly many, if not most, of the other families were making no adequate provision against serious illness or death of the breadwinner.

Life insurance was the most usual form of investment, carried by some person in every one of the seventy-seven families that reported any type of investment other than children's school savings. The average annual premiums paid per family were about $40 ($41.74 mean, $39 median). Usually the premiums amounted to less than $75 a year; seven families spent more. In the average family this amount covered life insurance premiums for four persons. Attempts to ascertain the face value of the policies proved futile,

TABLE 25

Expenditure for Investments during the Year

Annual expenditure	Number of families spending a specified amount				
	All investments	Insurance premiums	Savings		Other
			Family	Children	
All amounts...............	80*	77	25	16	3
Less than $25.00......	17	22	4	12	....
$25.00–$49.99...........	21	28	1	4	....
50.00– 74.99...........	14	20	3	....	....
75.00– 99.99...........	4	3	1	....	....
100.00–124.99...........	8	3	9	....	1
125.00–149.99...........	2	1	1	....	1
150.00–174.99...........	4	....	2	....	....
175.00–199.99...........	2	....	1	....	....
200.00–224.99...........	2	....	....	....	....
225.00–249.99...........	....	....	2	....	1
250.00–274.99...........	1	....	1	....	....
275.00–299.99...........	3	....	....	....	....
300.00–324.99...........	1	....	....	....	....
425.00–449.99...........	1	....	....	....	....
Average					
Mean...........................	$83.51	$41.74	$109.06	$14.74	$168.33
Median.......................	52.20	39.00	120.00	11.88	145.00

* Three of these families reported small amounts for children's savings and no other form of investment.

since most of the Mexicans were either ignorant or misinformed about the policy for which they were paying. The size of the premiums per person, however, makes it obvious that only burial insurance was carried in most cases. Those who carried no insurance were not, on the whole, protected by membership in mutual benefit associations. Only six of the twenty-five with no commercial insurance belonged to a lodge or a union and only one paid dues large enough to cover insurance premiums.

Twenty-five families reported bank savings for the year in addition to insurance premiums; the largest, $250; the most common estimate, $120 ($109.06 mean, $120 median). None of the families which made savings reported insurance premiums of more than $65. All but one of the families reporting bank savings had a total expenditure per consumption unit well above the average for the 100 families.

Two families bought lots within the year, and one invested $145 in stocks and bonds.

In an attempt to ascertain the circumstances which enabled these Mexicans to provide for the future, a comparison has been made between the twenty-three families with no investment or savings of any type within the year, or with only children's school savings, and the twenty-four families which reported amounts in excess of $100.[44]

The most striking differences between the two groups of families were that those which saved over $100 during the year had an average total expenditure per consumption unit twice as great as that of those families which saved nothing, and that, in the former group, twice as many heads of families were steadily employed throughout the year. In other words, the reports of appreciable savings came from those families which were most comfortably situated, with incomes comparatively steady and large in proportion to the number of persons in the family.

Such being the case, these families were able to save without unduly curtailing either necessaries or luxuries in their budget. The families which saved over $100 spent three times as much on leisure-time activities as those which saved nothing, and as high a proportion owned automobiles. Their expenditure per consumption unit for food was larger and the proportion of serious deficiencies smaller.

---

[44] That is, a total for the year of $100 for the category "investments," including life and accident insurance premiums, bank savings, stocks, real estate.

Because any serious illness among these Mexicans was cared for free or at greatly reduced rates, the costs of sickness do not appear as a major impediment to savings, as is often true in other groups. In this respect there was no appreciable difference between those with large savings and those with none.

The future of the twenty-three families without insurance or savings was not provided for by other forms of investment. Only one of the group owned or was buying a house, and only one paid mutual benefit dues large enough to provide insurance.

In brief, the Mexican families which made provision for the future were those with an available surplus after other needs had been supplied. One-fourth of the whole group carried no insurance and made no savings in this year. In the majority of cases there was little or no provision made beyond funeral costs.

Medical care.—It has become axiomatic that the poorest and the richest classes receive the best medical attention. As has already been mentioned, most of these Mexican families were eligible for free or part-pay medical care, and sixty-three reported receiving such care at some time in the year. Accordingly, sickness did not constitute such a drain on the budget as in working-class families of a higher income level, and there were few cases where a serious illness financially crippled the family.

Twenty-seven families reported no costs for medical care. Of these, seventeen received no attention whatever within the year and ten were cared for free of charge. Fifty-three others paid a part of their own costs, and twenty were entirely self-sustaining. In the latter families, which paid all their own costs of medical care, the amounts reported ranged from $3 to $82, the average less than $30 ($31.76 mean, $26.25 median). The average expenditure in the fifty-three families which received free or part-pay care was slightly higher ($41.81 mean, $30 median).

Taken together, seventy-three families which paid for part or all of their medical care spent an average of less than $40 a year ($39.06 mean, $30 median). The largest sum reported was $123. Of the ten families which spent more than $75, only one was unassisted by free or reduced-cost care. The only evidence of severe hardship arising from the cost of illness was in three families whose bills for medical care exceeded 10 per cent of the total family expenditure. In the schedule the costs of confinement were not separated from other medical expenses, but judging by the total bill for medical

TABLE 26

EXPENDITURE FOR MEDICAL CARE

Annual expenditure	Number of families spending a specified amount							
	All medical costs			Doctor	Dentist	Drugs	Hos-pital	Other
	All families	Paid in full	Paid part only*					
All amounts................	73	20	53	56	21	47	6	17
Less than $10.00.......	8	2	6	9	10	28	....	9
$10.00–$19.99............	17	5	12	13	7	16	....	5
20.00– 29.99............	11	4	7	14	1	1	....	2
30.00– 39.99............	9	2	7	8	2	1	1	1
40.00– 49.99............	7	3	4	5	....	....	....	....
50.00– 59.99............	4	2	2	2	1	....	2	....
60.00– 69.99............	2	....	2	3	....	....	....	....
70.00– 79.99............	6	1	5	....	....	....	2	....
80.00– 89.99............	3	1	2	....	....	....	1	....
90.00– 99.99............	2	....	2	....	....	1	....	....
100.00–109.99............	....	....	....	1	....	....	....	....
110.00–119.99............	1	....	1	1	....	....	....	....
120.00–129.99............	3	....	3	....	....	....	....	....
Average								
Mean............................	$39.06	$31.76	$41.81	$27.67	$12.90	$10.23	$60.83	$10.87
Median.........................	30.00	26.25	30.00	25.00	10.00	8.00	62.50	8.80

* This includes the total expenditure for medical care of all families which received any care at clinic rates. Some such families, of course, paid in full for all but one item, such as dentistry. The sum of this column is therefore greater than the total expenditure for clinical care, $938.55.

care in twenty-four families where a child was born within the year, the costs of childbirth averaged less than $50 and rarely exceeded $100. The most usual doctor's fee in such cases was $25. Eight, or one-third, of the confinements were in a hospital, three receiving free care and one reduced rates. Ten families paid the full costs of childbirth.

Of the $2851 spent for medical care during the year in this group of 100 families, $1549, 54 per cent, was spent for doctors; $481, 17 per cent, for drugs; $365, 13 per cent, for hospitals; $271, 10 per cent, for dentists; and the remainder, $185, 6 per cent, for miscellaneous items. Of the total amount, 33 per cent was only part-payment for the services received, and about half the families received completely free care in addition.

About half the families paid a small doctor's bill and bought some drugs within the year. One family in five paid a dentist's bill, and only six of the 100 paid anything for hospital care. Forty-three per cent of the dentists' bills, 34 per cent of the bills for doctors, 35 per cent of the miscellaneous bills, 28 per cent of the payments for drugs, and one of the six hospital bills, were only part-payment for the care received. Completely free hospital care, reported by nineteen families, was more common than part-pay; little free dental work was reported. It seems safe to assume that three-fourths of the Mexican children received no dental care within the year.

The average bill for the doctor was $25; for the dentist, $10; for drugs and for miscellaneous items such as eye-glasses, x-rays, and laboratory tests, less than $10. As has been already mentioned, the average total bill for medical care was less than $40 a year in those seventy-three families which paid anything for this item.

Associations.—Group activities, at least of societies which collected dues, played little part in the lives of these Mexicans. Less than half the families, forty-two, paid dues in any sort of association. Their situation differed sharply from that of Mexican immigrants in earlier studies and low-skilled labor in general. The *mutualistas*, societies combining mutual benefits for sickness and burial with social functions, and the variety of other social organizations noted by observers elsewhere,[45] were scarcely represented. Among the 100 families only four reported such memberships, two in the Unión Patriótica Benéfica Mexicana Independiente, one in

[45] Gamio, *Mexican immigration*, 131–136.

Taylor, Paul S., *Mexican labor in the United States* (University of California Press, 1930–1931), I: 62–64, 184–185, 359–360; II: 131–142.

the Alianza Hispano-Americana, and one in the Woodmen of the World. One belonged to a motorists' association, and six to purely social organizations with nominal dues.

On the other hand, thirty-two men belonged to some sort of union or employees' association, often with benefits attached, although the dues rarely exceeded 75 cents a month. This proportion is high for any group so predominantly low skilled or semi-skilled as this one. It is almost incredible for Mexicans, who, because of non-citizenship, are habitually excluded from unions associated with the American Federation of Labor. Some of these so-called union

TABLE 27

EXPENDITURE FOR ASSOCIATION DUES

Item	Number reporting	Average annual expenditure for families reporting	
		Mean	Median
All associations	42	$ 8.51	$ 9.00
Unions	32	7.84	9.00
Lodges, etc.—with insurance	4	17.58	18.30
Motorists' association	1	12.00	12.00
Social clubs, etc.	6	4.00	3.00

dues were paid to employees' associations with benefit features, as in the case of the six laborers working for the gas company and two working for the street car company. On the other hand, skilled trades unions were represented. The two cooks and the two barbers were union men, and two-thirds of the tailors and taxi or truck drivers. Five of the ten cement workers were union members, and three of the four fishermen and fish salesmen. The other seven union men were engaged in skilled or semi-skilled occupations.

None of the women, most of whom were employed irregularly in the canneries, reported union affiliations.

Education.—In eighty-two families there were children of school age, that is, six to sixteen. None of these children attended parochial or other private schools charging tuition, but some of them had small expenses for supplies in the public schools and some were taking music or dancing lessons. An occasional family reported costs for summer school, night school, or day nursery. Twenty-eight families reported at least one of these educational costs. Of the amounts spent, 36 per cent were less than $5; the highest was $122 ($29.79 mean, $18 median). Sixteen families, one in five of those

TABLE 28

EXPENDITURE FOR EDUCATIONAL ITEMS

Annual expenditure	Number of families spending a specified amount						
	All items	Public school expenses	Music or dancing lessons	Summer school	Night school	Day nursery	Parents' education
All amounts	28	16	13	3	2	3	2
Less than $25.00	16	16	7	3	2	....	2
Less than $5.00	10	10	....	....	2	....	2
$5.00–$9.99	1	2	....	....	....	....	....
10.00–14.99	....	4	1	....	....	....	....
15.00–19.99	5	....	6	2	....	....	....
20.00–24.99	....	....	....	1	....	....	....
$25.00–$49.99	6	....	2	....	....	2	....
50.00– 74.99	1	....	....	....	....	....	....
75.00– 99.99	3	....	3	....	....	1	....
100.00–124.99	2	....	1	....	....	....	....
Average							
Mean	$29.79	$4.98	$42.92	$17.50	$4.10	$45.00	$.30
Median	18.00	3.95	18.00	17.50	4.10	30.00	.30

with school children, reported minor expenses at public schools, for supplies, books, dues, etc. Such expenses averaged $4 to $5 per family and never exceeded $14. Thirteen families provided music or dancing lessons for their children at costs ranging from $10 to $120 a year ($42.92 mean, $18 median). Three families sent a child to summer school, of which the costs were $15 to $20. Two paid $3.70 and $4.50 respectively for grown sons at night school. Three wives, two of them gainfully employed, left young children at day nurseries for part of the year at an expenditure of $25, $30, and $80. Two families reported expenditures of less than $1 during the year for supplies in classes attended by the parents.

Charity.—All but fifteen of these Mexican families made contributions to dependent relatives, charitable causes, or the church.

TABLE 29

EXPENDITURE FOR CHARITY

Annual expenditure	Number of families spending a specified amount				
	Total charity	Dependents	Church	Charitable agencies	Other
All amounts.............	85	33	62	50	1
Less than $5.00........	32	1	30	47	....
$5.00–$9.99..............	10	1	14	3	....
10.00–14.99..............	9	4	15	....	....
15.00–19.99..............	9	9	2	....	....
20.00–24.99..............	7	5	1	....	....
25.00–29.99..............	6	5	....	....	....
30.00–34.99..............	3	3	....	....	....
35.00–39.99..............	3	....	....	....	....
40.00–44.99..............	3	2	....	....	....
45.00–49.99..............	....	....	....	....	1*
50.00–54.99..............	....	....	....	....	....
55.00–59.99..............	....	....	....	....	....
60.00–64.99..............	....	1	....	....	....
110.00–114.99...........	1	....	....	....	....
115.00–119.99...........	....	....	....	....	....
120.00–124.99...........	....	1	....	....	....
125.00–129.99...........	1	....	....	....	....
155.00–159.99...........	....	1	....	....	....
160.00–164.99...........	1	....	....	....	....
Average					
Mean..........................	$16.83	$28.15	$6.06	$1.62	....
Median.......................	10.00	20.00	5.00	1.00	....

* Gift to a sick friend.

The thirty-three families which contributed to dependents included three which sent regular allowances of $5 or $10 a month to a mother in Mexico. The others sent occasional sums, all less than $50 a year, to brothers, sisters, aunts, or more usually to parents. In almost every case these relatives were in Mexico. The average amount given to dependents was not large ($28.15 mean, $20 median) and the families which contributed were drawn, on the whole, from those with a total expenditure per consumption unit above the average.

Fifty families contributed to organized charity in small amounts, usually $1 or $2, never over $5 ($1.62 mean, $1 median). The average total expenditure per consumption unit was slightly higher in these families than in the group as a whole. One family gave $45 to a sick friend.

The contributions to church of sixty-two families ranged from 25 cents to $24, averaging $5 or $6 a year. The families which contributed apparently did so regardless of the amount of their incomes.

There was no tendency to consider one of these forms of charity as a substitute for the other. Families which gave to organized charity were as likely to contribute to the church and to the support of dependents as were those which did not.

Other expenses.—Sixty-three families reported items not included in the above categories. Thirty-six reported lump sums for unitemized "incidentals," ranging from $6 to $30 and averaging $16. Twenty-four repaid debts contracted in previous years. Three of these amounts exceeded $100; half were less than $50. Ten loaned money to others, eight reporting sums of $50 or less, and one of $250. Six paid for funerals that cost between $10 and $175. In five families the man was working away from home for part of the year and had to pay board and lodging in amounts between $30 and $240. Five other families reported miscellaneous small expenses.

TABLE 30

EXPENDITURE FOR SPECIFIED RESIDUAL ITEMS

Annual expenditure	Number of families spending a specified amount					
	Incidentals	Debts repaid	Loans to others	Funerals	Board and lodging —man	Other expenses
All amounts...............	36	24	10	6	5	5
Less than $25.00.........	33	3	4	1	....	4
Less than $5.00.......	....	....	....	....	....	1
$5.00–$9.99..............	1	....	1	....	....	....
10.00–14.99..............	12	2	2	1	....	1
15.00–19.99..............	6	....	1	....	....	2
20.00–24.99..............	14	1	....	....	....	....
$25.00–$49.99..............	3	9	3	3	3	1
50.00– 74.99..............	....	4	1	....	....	....
75.00– 99.99..............	....	5	....	....	....	....
100.00–124.99..............	....	....	1	....	....	....
125.00–149.99..............	....	....	....	1	....	....
150.00–174.99..............	....	....	....	....	....	....
175.00–199.99..............	....	1	....	1	....	....
200.00–224.99..............	....	1	....	....	1	....
225.00–249.99..............	....	....	....	....	1	....
250.00–274.99..............	....	....	1	....	....	....
275.00–299.99..............	....	....	....	....	....	....
300.00–324.99..............	....	1	....	....	....	....
Average						
Mean..............................	$16.28	$68.77	$58.10	$70.00	$111.70	$17.57
Median............................	16.50	45.00	35.00	37.50	48.00	15.00

VI

SUMMARY

The typical Mexican family.—The typical family in the group of Mexicans studied consisted of father, mother, and three or four children under sixteen, the parents born in Mexico, the children in California. The man was usually engaged in low-skilled or semi-skilled work, earning about $1000 a year. In a trifle less than half the cases the woman was gainfully employed, usually in a cannery, for part of the year. The children, on the whole, were still dependent. The average family had income to supplement the man's earnings from some source, such as wife's or children's earnings, or contributions from relatives, which raised its total money income to about $1300 a year. In addition, the average family received income in kind—food, second-hand clothing, firewood, free or part-pay medical care. Approximately half the families broke even at the end of the year, half ran slightly behind.

The costs of food amounted to one-third of the average family expenditure, about $500 a year, but this was insufficient to provide a minimum standard diet. On the whole, these people still clung to their native Mexican food habits—beans and tortillas, few vegetables or dairy products. American clothes, on the contrary, had entirely replaced Mexican dress. The average family spent about $50 each for the husband's and wife's clothing each year and about $25 for each child. The total clothing expenditure amounted to 13 per cent. The average family was much better housed than would have been possible in Mexico, although overcrowding prevailed. For $20 a month it rented a three- or four-room house with bathroom and toilet, electricity, and gas. The majority of families did not have a washing machine, a telephone, household service even in times of illness, ice, or commercial laundry service, although laundry bills were reported in a surprisingly large number of families, marking the progress of Americanization. Less than half the families were buying furniture on the installment plan and the payments were not unduly heavy. Men and children had their hair cut by the barber.

The typical family found its chief recreation in the movies, with occasional patronage of some other form of commercial amusement, bought a newspaper, gave the children about $1 a month for candy and ice cream, spent $20 a year for the man's tobacco. Between 5 and 6 per cent of the average family budget was devoted to leisure-time activities. One family in four was buying a radio. One family in four owned a second-hand automobile which cost $10 a month to operate. The others spent $1 to $2 a month for carfare. The average family apparently had little set aside for illness or the death of the breadwinner. It carried burial insurance policies on four persons, with total annual premiums of $40. One-fourth of the families saved about $10 a month during the year; one-fourth made no provision of any sort for the future. The costs of illness were not a heavy burden, since the average family received part of its medical care free or at reduced rates, and thus spent only $40 a year. Most of this went to doctors. Dentistry was obviously neglected.

One-third of the men belonged to unions or employees' associations, very few to mutual benefit societies or purely social organizations. Expenses for school or lessons were rare. The average family contributed small amounts to church and to charity. One-third of the families sent small money gifts to relatives in Mexico. One-fourth were repaying debts contracted in previous years.

On the whole these Mexican families, typically immigrants though they were, had adopted the American standard of living to a large extent, with the notable exception of their diet. The chief examples of this tendency were the clothing worn, the good housing conditions, and the fact that 30 per cent of the average budget went for items other than the "necessaries" of food, clothing, and shelter.

VII

COMPARISON WITH OTHER COST OF LIVING STUDIES

The preceding sections have outlined the way of living of an immigrant working-class group, in so far as it is represented by the expenditures of a year. The following pages show the similarities and differences between the Mexicans' habits of expenditure and those of a number of other working-class groups in this country and of one group of federal employees in Mexico.

Six working-class groups have been selected: two studied twenty-five years ago—New York tenement dwellers and Pennsylvania steel workers; those in a country-wide study of wage earners in 1918–19; and those in three recent studies of unskilled and semi-skilled workers in Oakland, California, in Chicago, and in the Ford plant at Detroit. In all but one of these groups the income was higher than that of the average Mexican family in the present study, allowing for changes in price levels, and the family was smaller in every case, putting the Mexicans at an additional economic disadvantage. The study of Treasury employees in Mexico was chosen as being the only adequate cost of living investigation in that country in recent years, although for our purpose a study of a group of wage earners would have been more satisfactory.

Comparison with the older studies shows the growth of secondary wants, such as automobiles, radios, and movies, that has taken place in the last twenty years. The emphasis of Mexican spending is for these new wants at the expense of food, housing, and savings. The other recent studies show the same trend, but tend, with larger incomes, to provide more fully for the necessaries of life before money is spent for amusements. A larger percentage of Mexicans reported substandard food expenditures than is found in any other study, except perhaps in that of 1918–19 where it was impossible to make a direct comparison. More overcrowding is found among the Mexicans than in any other group except the New York City

residents. On the other hand, the growing public control of sanitation and the spread of modern housing conveniences in California
have made the Mexicans better off in these respects than families
in earlier studies. The Mexican families appear to be less thrifty.
They reported less insurance or savings and fewer affiliations with
organizations that offer benefit features. The proximity to Mexico
and the possibility of a return there in case of want may afford a
partial explanation.

New York City, 1907—workingmen.[46]—Twenty-five years ago
Robert Chapin made a study of the "essentials and cost of a normal
standard of living" for the New York State Conference of Charities
and Corrections, for which 391 expenditure records were gathered
from workingmen's families in New York City. The families included were limited to those with not less than two or more than
four children under sixteen, and preferably with incomes from $500
to $1000.[47] The sample was predominantly of European immigrants,
who constituted 70 per cent of those studied, but it did not represent any single national group. Because of the qualifications set up
for inclusion in the study, the average family of 5 persons, was
slightly smaller than the average Mexican family of 5.6 persons.
As always in large cities, lodgers were more common in the New
York study, reported by 34 per cent of the families, as contrasted
with 2 per cent of the Mexican families in the present study.

A combination of the cost of living index in Douglas' *Real Wages
in the United States, 1890-1926* and the current index of the United
States Bureau of Labor Statistics shows that the general price level
for the country as a whole in terms of the consumer's dollar was
some 75 per cent higher in 1929–30 than in 1907. On this basis,
and making no allowance for price differences due to locality, the
purchasing power of an income of $800 in 1907, the average for the
New York families, was about $1400 in 1929–30. The average
Mexican family's income was about $1300.

---

[46] Chapin, Robert C., *The standard of living among workingmen's families in
New York City*, Russell Sage Foundation (1909).

[47] Following Chapin's example we quote figures for only 318 families which
had incomes between $600 and $1100.

The man's earnings constituted a higher proportion of the family income, 89 per cent, in the New York families than among the Mexicans, 80 per cent. Eighteen per cent of the New York women were gainfully employed within the year in contrast to 43 per cent of the Mexican women. Apparently families with children over sixteen were excluded from the New York study, so that children's earnings were a minor factor in the family income.

TABLE 31

PERCENTAGE DISTRIBUTION OF EXPENDITURES BY NEW YORK
WORKINGMEN'S FAMILIES—CHAPIN, 1907—COMPARED WITH
MEXICANS

Items	Percentage of total expenditure excluding savings*	
	New York workingmen	San Diego Mexicans
Total expenditure	100.0	100.0
Food	44.8	37.6
Clothing	14.0	14.0
Housing	20.8	16.4
Fuel and light	5.1	2.7
Insurance	2.4†	2.4
Medical care	2.2	2.1
Carfare	1.7	1.5
Other	9.0	23.3

* Regardless of the number of families reporting each item.
† Includes property insurance, excludes insurance carried by mutual benefit associations.

Comparison of the percentage distribution of expenditures in the two studies shows a marked divergence of spending habits, partly caused, perhaps, by local conditions and by shifts in relative prices since 1907, but attributable in great part to changes in wants and standards of living in the intervening twenty years. The Mexicans spent relatively less for food, housing, and fuel—the "necessaries" —and devoted nearly one-fourth of their total expenditure to those items which Chapin could afford to dismiss as "sundries," a category which includes the cost of an automobile, of all leisure-time and educational activities, association dues, charity, barber and cosmetics and personal cleaning supplies, furnishings, and all costs of operating the house other than fuel and light. This shift in the emphasis of expenditure exemplifies the changes which have occurred over this span of years. In 1907 the automobile was a new invention, purchased only by those with large incomes; by 1930 it was within the price range of one in every four Mexican workmen. In 1907 the radio had not yet been invented nor moving pictures perfected. The chief forms of recreation reported by the families in Chapin's study were excursions and lodge meetings. Many families reported no other form of recreation than visiting with relatives or neighbors. Twenty years later, low-priced radios were being bought on the installment plan, and the "talkies" had become the chief source of entertainment for all classes and ages, so much so that the majority of Mexican families spent for them more than $1 a month in addition to occasional patronage of other commercial amusements. Not only new inventions, but also the growth of installment selling and easy credit, the manufacturers' policy of developing new markets among the lower-income groups, and the effect of advertising in creating a demand for small luxuries, have all played their part in the changed direction of expenditure, which includes not only greater allowances for all forms of recreation, but also increased expenditures for furnishings, children's lessons, charities, and minor miscellaneous expenses.

The Mexicans obtained the surplus to spend on these "cultural" wants by reducing their proportional expenditures for food, housing, and fuel. Rents are higher in New York than in other parts of the country and more fuel is required on the Atlantic seaboard than in California. Although the New York families devoted a larger proportion of their total income to housing, overcrowding was as prevalent there as among the Mexicans, approximately half of each group falling below Chapin's standard of one and one-half persons per room. Housing conditions were probably better among the Mexicans, despite their lower proportional expenditure, because they escaped many of the evils attendant upon overcrowding by living in a small city almost suburban in character, with mild winters, and enjoyed the benefits of modern household conveniences and sanitation. It is important to remember that many conveniences which were seldom seen in 1907 had become common by 1929 —in particular, electricity and sanitary appliances. It is thus only to be expected that none of the families studied in 1907 had electricity and only three-fourths had gas for lighting, whereas 90 per cent of the Mexican dwellings were lighted by electricity; and only 18 per cent of the New York families had private baths and only 27 per cent had private toilets, in marked contrast to the 60 per cent and 70 per cent respectively among the Mexicans.

The New York families were better fed than the Mexicans. Chapin employed a standard to measure the adequacy of food expenditures which, after allowance is made for price changes, did not differ substantially from that used in the present study. He found 23 per cent of the New York families underfed, a contrast to 76 per cent of the Mexicans.

Data are lacking to make a direct comparison of the thriftiness of the two groups,[48] but apparently they made about the same provision for the future. Approximately three-fourths of both groups were paying life insurance premiums,[49] amounting to no more than burial insurance in the majority of cases, and about one-fourth reported savings for the year.

Chapin concludes that "an income of $900 or over probably permits the maintenance of a normal standard, at least so far as the physical man is concerned." The equivalent of the purchasing power of $900 in 1907 would be approximately $1600 in 1929–30. Only one Mexican family in four reported an income of this amount, yet the emphasis of Mexican spending was in the direction of those "higher wants," especially various forms of diversion, which are supposed to be a prerogative of much larger incomes.

---

[48] Since Chapin classified savings and investment as surplus, not as an item of expenditure, they have been omitted from the Mexican expenditures in table 31.

[49] This includes thirty-four families in the New York study and one in the Mexican which belonged to mutual benefit associations and therefore did not buy commercial insurance.

Homestead, Pennsylvania, 1907-8—mill hands.[50]—At the time
when Chapin was studying the cost of living in New York, the
Pittsburgh Survey of the Russell Sage Foundation was engaged in
an investigation of the living conditions of steel workers in Homestead, Pennsylvania, in the course of which household accounts
were collected from ninety families. Of these, 28 per cent were
native white, 26 per cent Negro, 32 per cent Slav, and the remainder English, Scotch, Irish, and German immigrants. The
average Homestead family was smaller by one child than the average Mexican family in the San Diego study. One family in five
took in lodgers, contrasted to one family in fifty among the
Mexicans.

The average weekly expenditure shown by the account books was
$15.50,[51] the equivalent of $1400 per annum in 1929–30—about
$50 a year higher than the average total expenditure of the Mexican
families. No measure is available for difference in price levels
resulting from difference of locality. Only 10 per cent of the wives
were gainfully employed within the year. Families in which the
man's earnings were low more commonly supplemented their
income by taking lodgers.

As with the New York families, the principal difference in the
distribution of expenditures of mill hands and Mexicans was the
difference in emphasis on leisure-time activities and other secondary
wants. This may result not only from those factors already considered in connection with the Chapin study, but also from the
fact that the Homestead group was suffering at the time from
under-employment and was forced to certain economies in its usual
scale of living. The proportion spent on housing was the same in
both groups; the Mexicans' relative allowance for food was slightly
less. Since the Homestead families' real purchasing power was
greater, especially with normal employment, there was less undernourishment and overcrowding. Applying the same standard food
allowance as was used by Chapin, we find that 23 per cent of the
Homestead families, the same proportion as in New York, were

[50] Byington, Margaret F., *Homestead*, Russell Sage Foundation (1910).
[51] Many of the accounts were kept during a period of depression and unemployment. The average family income per week was normally $18.

spending less than the minimum requirement for adequate nourishment. Of the Mexican families, 76 per cent fell below the Chapin standard. Fifty-six per cent of the Homestead families met the standard of at least one room per person, in contrast to 20 per cent of the Mexicans. As appeared in contrasting the New York families with the Mexicans, the developments of twenty years had greatly

TABLE 32

PERCENTAGE DISTRIBUTION OF EXPENDITURES BY HOMESTEAD
MILL HANDS—BYINGTON, 1907-8—COMPARED
WITH MEXICANS

Item	Percentage of total expenditure excluding savings*	
	Homestead mill hands	San Diego Mexicans
Total expenditure............................	100.0	100.0
Food..	40.7	37.6
Clothing..	12.0	14.0
Housing..	16.5	16.4
Fuel and light.................................	4.1	2.7
Minor household expenses............	2.5	3.1
Furnishings......................................	2.1	2.7
Insurance...	6.4	2.4
Medical care...................................	2.4	2.1
Tobacco..	0.4	1.2
Liquor...	1.8	†
Other...	11.1	17.8

* Regardless of the number of families reporting each item.

† The purchases of wine or beer reported in a few Mexican families were classified as food expenses. Probably some of the money reported as "incidentals" was spent for liquor.

improved sanitary conditions. Nearly half the Homestead families had no running water in the house; only one in six had an indoor water-closet; bathrooms were rare.

The mill families spent nearly three times as high a proportion of their income for insurance as did the Mexicans. This may be partly attributable to the fact that the men were engaged in a highly hazardous occupation in the days before workmen's compensation laws had been adopted.

United States, 1918–19—wage earners and small-salaried men.[52]— The largest contemporary study in the field of cost of living was made by the United States Bureau of Labor Statistics in 1918–19, covering 12,096 families of wage earners and small-salaried men in ninety-two cities. Seventy-five per cent of the inquiries covered the calendar year 1918. It differed from the Mexican study in excluding all families keeping boarders or having older children who paid board, "slum" families, and non-English-speaking families which had been less than five years in the country. Elimination of families with older children who paid board and lodging naturally tended to exclude the larger households. The average family contained five persons, smaller by one-half person than the average Mexican family in the present study.

The cost of living index of the Bureau of Labor Statistics showed a decrease of 7 per cent between the years 1918[53] and 1929–30. The average total expenditure in the government study, excluding savings and investments which are listed as surplus, was $1434. Corrected for the lower purchasing power of the dollar, the expenditures of the government families were no larger than those of the average Mexican family (mean total expenditure $1348),[54] but there were fewer mouths to feed. Less than 1 per cent of the average income was derived from the earnings of the wives, in contrast to 9 per cent in the average Mexican family.

The percentage distribution of expenditures shows a much closer similarity to the Mexicans' spending habits than appeared in the Chapin and Homestead studies. Expenditures for certain items differ widely, but the emphasis on items other than food, clothing, and shelter so characteristic of the Mexicans also appears in the families studied in 1918–19.

---

[52] United States Bureau of Labor Statistics, Bulletin 357, *Cost of living in the United States* (1924).

[53] The year covered by most of the schedules in the government study was approximately the calendar year 1918. This and succeeding figures on changes in the cost of living are taken from the United States Bureau of Labor Statistics index which appears semi-annually in the *Monthly Labor Review.*

[54] Excluding savings and investments.

TABLE 33

PERCENTAGE DISTRIBUTION OF EXPENDITURES BY WAGE-EARNERS' FAMILIES
IN THE UNITED STATES—UNITED STATES BUREAU OF LABOR STATISTICS,
1918-19—COMPARED WITH MEXICANS

Item	Percentage of total expenditure excluding savings*			
	United States wage earners		San Diego Mexicans	
Total expenditure	100.0		100.0	
Food	38.2		37.6	
Clothing	16.6		14.0	
Housing	13.0†		16.4	
House operation	7.6		5.8	
Fuel and light		5.2†		2.7
Other household expenses		2.4		3.1
Furnishings	4.5‡		2.7	
Care of person	1.0		2.6	
Automobile, motorcycle, bicycle	1.1		3.1	
Other transportation	1.9		1.9	
Insurance	3.0		2.4	
Medical care	4.2		2.1	
Leisure time	4.7		6.6	
Reading matter		0.7		0.4
Commercial amusements		0.8		1.7
Musical instruments		0.8		1.2
Vacation		0.5		0.3
Tobacco		1.2		1.2
Other		0.7		1.8
Associations	0.5		0.3	
Education	0.5		0.6	
School expenses		0.3		0.2
Lessons		0.2¶		0.4
Philanthropy	0.8§		1.1	
Church		0.7		0.3
Charity		0.1		0.1
Dependents		§		0.7
Other	1.8		2.8	

* Regardless of the number reporting each item.

† Three hundred and one families in which rent was combined with fuel and light are omitted.

‡ *Tools* have been added to the original class, "furnishings," and *musical instruments* moved to "leisure time."

¶ Only "music" is listed in the government study. Either no other types of lessons were purchased, or they have been included in "other miscellaneous."

§ Donations to dependents outside the home are apparently included in "gifts" which are classified under "leisure time—other."

TABLE 34

AVERAGE (MEAN) EXPENDITURE PER FAMILY REPORTING FOR CERTAIN SIG-
NIFICANT ITEMS BY WAGE-EARNERS' FAMILIES IN THE UNITED STATES—UNITED
STATES BUREAU OF LABOR STATISTICS, 1918–19—COMPARED WITH MEXICANS

Item	Percentage reporting		Mean annual expenditure per family reporting	
	United States wage earners	San Diego Mexicans	United States wage earners	San Diego Mexicans
Food	100	100	$548.51	$506.58
Clothing	100	100	237.60	188.50
Housing	*	98	186.55	225.57
Fuel and light	*	98	74.28	37.19
Cleaning supplies	100	100	12.15	20.88
Laundry sent out	70	59	17.91	24.54
Telephone	28	29	16.35	9.20
Service	16	8	25.04	24.00
Barber	96	95	7.87	14.44
Personal cleaning supplies	99	96	6.50	21.56
Automobile, motorcycle, bicycle	15	26	105.77	159.40
Carfare	89	98	27.02	20.60
Insurance	90	77	48.38	41.74
Doctor	86	56	37.33	27.67
Dentist	46	21	17.77	12.90
Hospital	11	6	42.76	60.83
Newspapers	96	52	8.17	7.98
Movies	78	82	10.07	18.07
Vacation	26	12	28.97	39.33
Tobacco	80	75	20.59	21.91
Union dues	31	30	14.93	7.96
Other association dues†	29	13	11.83	9.10
Music and other lessons‡	13	13	19.83	42.92
Church	72	62	14.15	6.06
Charity	30	51	4.49	2.48

* Two and one-half per cent of the families, where rent was combined with fuel and light, are omitted.
† Lodge dues which were primarily insurance premiums were included under the latter heading by the Bureau.
‡ See note, table 33.

Undernourishment, according to our standards, must have been widely prevalent in the wage-earning class at the close of the war. If food expenditures in the 1918–19 study are reduced to a 1929–30 basis, the Mexicans, who were markedly underfed and whose families were only slightly larger, spent slightly more for food. The Mexicans spent a higher proportion of their total budget on rent and reported more overcrowding, possibly because rents throughout the whole country increased 45 per cent from 1918 to 1929–30. The average 1918–19 family met the standard of one room per person. The characteristically high allowance of the Mexicans for leisure-time activities exceeded that of the average family in 1918–19. The average Mexican expenditure for commercial amusements was twice as large and musical instruments were more common, half of the purchases being radios, in contrast to pianos and phonographs ten years before. Nearly all the families studied in 1918–19 bought newspapers; only half the Mexicans, who also bought fewer magazines and books. Ownership of automobiles has, of course, tremendously increased since the war. Fifteen per cent of the families studied in 1918–19 owned automobiles, motorcycles, or bicycles. Twenty-six per cent of the Mexicans owned automobiles; one also had a bicycle. The Mexicans spent more on their cars.

The Mexicans made less provision for death, old age, or emergencies. Ninety per cent of the families studied in 1918–19 carried life or accident insurance, 77 per cent of the Mexicans. Savings and investments were classified as surplus in the earlier study, appearing in 70 per cent of the families and averaging $155 for each family reporting. Thirty-eight per cent of the Mexicans reported savings or investments, an average of $91 per family.

The families in the 1918–19 study spent 4 per cent of their budget on medical care, the Mexicans only 2 per cent. A greater proportion of families in the former study reported doctors' and dentists' bills. This may reflect, to some extent, the growth of free medical care in the intervening twelve years. Ninety-nine per cent of the 1918–19 families, however, reported expenditures for some sort of medical care, whereas 17 per cent of the Mexicans had no medical attention, either free or paid.

Oakland, California, 1924-25—street-car men.[55]—Five years previous to the present study the Heller Committee made a similar

---

[55] Heller Committee for Research in Social Economics, *Spending ways of a semi-skilled group*, Univ. Calif. Publ. Econ., 5 (1931): 295–366.

investigation of the incomes and expenditures of ninety-eight families of men employed on the local street and interurban electric railways and belonging to the Amalgamated Association of Street and Electrical Railway Employees.

The group was predominantly of native American and English-speaking stock. The average family in this group contained slightly more than two dependent children in contrast to the three or four children in the typical Mexican family investigated.[56] Twenty-two carmen's families reported boarders and lodgers, only two of the Mexican families. The street-car men's families included nine children who paid board.

The Bureau of Labor Statistics' cost of living index for San Francisco and Oakland showed practically no change between 1924–25 and 1929–30, so that the factor of shifting price levels may be disregarded in comparing the incomes of the two groups.[57]

The average income of street-car men's families was about $1800; the average Mexican family's income was about $1300. Only sixteen of the carmen's wives were employed within the year, forty-three of the Mexican women. The carmen's earnings formed a greater proportion of the total family income than did the earnings of Mexican men.

The percentage distribution of expenditure was strikingly similar in the two groups—37 per cent for food, 16 to 18 per cent for housing, 11 to 14 per cent for clothing, 6 per cent for house operation, and 3 per cent for furnishings, leaving one-fourth of the total expenditure for other items.

Since the Mexicans' total expenditure was only two-thirds as great as that of the street-car men and since their families were larger, the diversion of 25 per cent to secondary items left them obviously less well provided with necessaries. In the face of approximately equivalent food prices and an average family larger by 1.6 persons than the average carman's family, the Mexicans were

---

[56] The Mexican study excluded childless families, of which there were six among the street-car men.

[57] No figures are available for San Diego. It is impossible to measure the differences in living costs between the two localities, but it seems fair to assume that they are not very great.

TABLE 35

AVERAGE EXPENDITURE PER FAMILY REGARDLESS OF THE NUMBER REPORTING
AND PERCENTAGE DISTRIBUTION OF EXPENDITURE BY OAKLAND STREET-CAR
MEN—HELLER COMMITTEE, 1924–25—COMPARED WITH MEXICANS

Item	Average annual expenditure per family		Percentage of total expenditure	
	Oakland street-car men	San Diego Mexicans	Oakland street-car men	San Diego Mexicans
Total expenditure	$2109.40	$1382.68	100.0	100.0
Food	790.65	506.58	37.5	36.6
Clothing	239.69	188.50	11.3	13.6
Men	$88.25	$52.02	4.2	3.8
Women	68.83	50.98	3.2	3.7
Children	82.03	83.45	3.9	6.0
Dependents	.58	2.05	......	0.1
Housing	373.19	221.06	17.7	16.0
House operation	123.89	78.74	5.9	5.7
Light and fuel	75.05	36.44	3.6	2.6
Cleaning supplies	12.23*	20.88	0.6	1.5
Laundry sent out	19.82	14.48	0.9	1.1
Telephone	7.33	2.67	0.3	0.2
Other	9.46	4.27	0.5	0.3
Furniture and furnishings	74.32	36.42	3.5	2.6
Care of the person	33.42	34.42	1.6	2.5
Barber	13.43	13.72	0.6	1.0
Personal cleaning supplies	19.99	20.70	1.0	1.5
Leisure time	126.41	89.54	6.0	6.5
Reading matter	10.00	5.28	0.5	0.4
Commercial amusements	36.12	22.75	1.7	1.6
Vacations	25.32	4.72	1.2	0.4
Tobacco	17.59	16.43	0.8	1.2
Allowances to children	3.98	9.95	0.2	0.7
Gifts	26.15	6.03	1.2	0.4
Other	7.25	24.38	0.4	1.8
Automobile	55.85	41.26	2.7	3.0
Other transportation	23.64	25.78	1.1	1.9
Investments	110.46	66.81	5.2	4.8
Insurance	51.28	32.14	2.4	2.3
Investments and savings	59.18	34.67	2.8	2.5
Medical care	86.89	28.51	4.1	2.1
Associations	32.88	3.57	1.6	0.3
Unions	18.14	2.39	0.9	0.2
Other	14.74	1.18	0.7	0.1
Education	10.28	8.34	0.5	0.6
Tuition, supplies, etc.	5.82	2.76	0.3	0.2
Lessons	4.46	5.58	0.2	0.4
Charity	12.66	14.31	0.6	1.0
Dependents	4.10	9.29	0.2	0.6
Church	6.62	3.76	0.3	0.3
Charity	1.94	1.26	0.1	0.1
Other	15.17	38.84	0.7	2.8

* Thirty-three families were unable to separate these items from the total grocery bill.

spending nearly $300 a year less for food. The available data indicate that only 4 per cent of the carmen's families were spending less than the standard allowance for food, in contrast to 76 per cent of

TABLE 36

Average (Mean) Expenditure per Family Reporting for Certain Significant Items by Oakland Street-car Men—Heller Committee, 1924-25 —Compared with Mexicans

Item	Number reporting		Mean annual expenditure per family reporting	
	Oakland street-car men	San Diego Mexicans	Oakland street-car men	San Diego Mexicans
House cleaning and laundry supplies..............	65*	100	$ 18.44	$ 20.88
Laundry sent out........................	58	59	33.49	24.54
Telephone†................................	34	29	21.12	9.20
Automobile................................	29	26	188.73	158.68
Insurance...................................	89	77	56.47	41.74
Investments and savings...........	65	38	89.23	91.24
Reading matter...........................	84	61	11.66	8.66
Commercial amusements............	93	88	38.07	25.85
Vacation....................................	24	12	103.40	39.33
Tobacco.....................................	62	75	27.80	21.91
Allowances to children...............	18	71	21.69	14.01
Gifts...	89	56	28.69	10.77
Church.......................................	55	62	11.80	6.06
Charity.......................................	83	51	2.29	2.48
Dependents................................	6	33	67.00	28.15
School expenses, etc...................	33	23	17.30	12.00
Lessons—music, etc....................	11	13	39.68	42.92
Union dues.................................	98	30	18.14	7.96
Other association dues...............	59	13	24.49	9.10

* The other families were unable to separate these items from the total grocery bill.
† Twenty-four street-car men's families and seven Mexicans had regular telephone service.

the Mexicans. Housing conditions among the Mexicans were notably poorer. Only one family in five achieved the standard of one room per person, which was met in two-thirds of the street-car men's families. Nearly half of the latter owned or were buying their homes, in contrast to 13 per cent of the Mexican families.

The Mexicans achieved great economies in the cost of fuel by gathering free wood; very few had telephones; otherwise, little difference is to be perceived in the costs of house operation for the two groups.

The Mexicans spent 6.5 per cent, $90, for leisure-time activities, the carmen 6 per cent, or $126. Of these items, vacations, gifts, and reading matter were more important in the budgets of the street-car men. Despite a lower income, as many Mexicans as street-car men owned automobiles,[58] and the costs were nearly as large.

Like most immigrants, the Mexicans had a greater burden of dependency. One-third contributed to the support of relatives, usually in Mexico. Only six of the ninety-eight street-car men reported such expenses.

As a group the carmen paid in full for their medical care; the Mexicans did not. This item amounted to 4 per cent of the average carman's budget, $87, and only 2 per cent, $29, for the average Mexican family.

The Mexicans were less well provided against death or economic disaster. Fewer families carried life insurance or saved money during the year, fewer belonged to unions or associations which might have benefit features, whereas every street-car man belonged at least to the union.

Chicago, 1924-25—unskilled laborers.[59]—Almost simultaneously with the Oakland study an investigation was made in Chicago of the incomes and standard of living of unskilled laborers as a check on the minimum budget in use by charitable agencies. These families were mainly immigrants; the majority were Poles or other Slavs and Italians. They differed from the San Diego Mexicans in having, on the average, only two or three dependent children instead of three or four, and in having fewer dependent relatives in the household.

---

[58] A study of the carmen in 1929–30 might show an increased proportion of automobile owners.

[59] Houghteling, Leila, *The income and standard of living of unskilled laborers in Chicago* (1927).

The median income of the Chicago families was $400 higher than the Mexicans',[60] $1674 as against $1274. Fewer wives were at work and more children were contributing to the family income. Unfortunately the method employed in this study does not permit a general comparison of the distribution of expenditures, but only of certain items.

Both smaller incomes and poorer dietary habits affected the Mexicans' food expenditures. Seventy-six per cent of the Mexican families fell below the standard allowance for food, and only 43 per cent of the Chicago families.[61] In both cases about one family in ten reported food expenditures more than 50 per cent below standard. The Chicago families spent 39 per cent of their total budget for food, the Mexicans only 37 per cent. A detailed analysis of the food purchases of a selected group of Chicago families showed that even when expenditures for food exceeded the standard, 63 per cent of the diets were inadequate in two, three, or four essentials. Examination of menus and of articles purchased makes it seem improbable that the twenty-two Mexican families which spent more than the standard allotment bettered this record.

The Mexicans likewise had less house room. Only 20 per cent reached or exceeded the standard of one room per person, in contrast to 33 per cent of the Chicago families. On the other hand, 78 per cent of the Mexicans had the use of a private bathroom, as against only 42 per cent of the Chicago families. Electricity for lighting was much more common in San Diego. Both groups spent about the same percentage of their total budget for rent. Twice as great a proportion of Chicagoans owned or were buying their homes, in spite of the greater size of the city.

Approximately the same proportion of families in both studies reported savings.

Detroit, 1929—Ford employees.[62]—Early in 1930 the United States Bureau of Labor Statistics made an investigation of the living con-

[60] As previously mentioned, there was no appreciable change in the cost of living between 1924–25 and 1929–30. No measure of the difference in living costs between Chicago and San Diego is available.

[61] The same food standard, adjusted to local prices, was used in both cases.

[62] "Standard of living of employees of the Ford Motor Co. in Detroit," *Monthly Labor Review*, XXX (1930): 1209–1252.

ditions and expenses of 100 Ford Motor Company employees in Detroit during 1929. Families included were limited to those in which the man worked at least 225 days in 1929 and earned approximately $7 a day, and in which there was no material income other than his earnings. The families included two or three children under sixteen, no older children, boarders, lodgers, or relatives, and had no outside dependents.

Because of the narrow limits set by these specifications, the average family consisted of 4.5 persons, of whom 2.5 were children under sixteen, and had an income of $1712, of which 99 per cent was the man's earnings. The average Mexican family in San Diego had one more child, and a number of families included older children or relatives. The average income of the Detroit group was $1712, or $375 a year more than the Mexicans' average. Nearly half the Mexican women were employed at some time in the year; families in which the woman was employed were excluded from the Detroit study.

The percentage distributions of expenditures by the two groups were closely similar, but there were greater differences than appeared between the Mexicans and the Oakland street-car men. Although any costs of purchasing a house which exceeded its rental value were classified as savings in the Detroit study, and thus excluded from expenditure, the proportion spent for housing by Ford employees was much greater than that spent by the Mexicans. The colder climate of Detroit necessitated much larger expenditures for fuel. The proportional expenditure for automobiles and for medical care was also greater in the Detroit study. The Mexicans, on the other hand, spent a much higher proportion of their total budget for leisure-time activities.

Analysis of the food purchases of the Ford employees indicated that "the food consumption of the Detroit families was, on the average, sufficient in quantity and well balanced as regards the important constituents of protein, calcium, phosphorus, and iron." Leaving out of consideration differences in price level between Detroit and San Diego,[63] the average Detroit family exceeded the

---

[63] No doubt such differences exist, but exact measures of them are lacking.

TABLE 37

AVERAGE EXPENDITURE PER FAMILY REGARDLESS OF THE NUMBER REPORTING AND PERCENTAGE DISTRIBUTION OF EXPENDITURE BY FORD EMPLOYEES IN DETROIT—UNITED STATES BUREAU OF LABOR STATISTICS, 1929—COMPARED WITH MEXICANS

Item	Average annual expenditure per family		Percentage of total expenditure	
	Ford employees	San Diego Mexicans	Ford employees	San Diego Mexicans
Total expenditure*	$1719.83	$1348.01	100.0	100.0
Food	549.18	506.58	31.9	37.6
Clothing	210.67	188.50	12.2	14.0
Husband	63.59	52.02	3.7	3.9
Wife	59.21	50.98	3.4	3.8
Children	87.87	85.50†	5.1	6.3
Housing	390.59‡	221.06	22.7	16.4
House operation	136.56	78.74	7.9	5.8
Fuel and light	103.20	36.44	6.0	2.7
Cleaning supplies	16.64	20.88	1.0	1.5
Laundry sent out	4.23	14.48	0.2	1.1
Telephone	1.71	2.67	0.1	0.2
Service	1.08	1.92	0.1	0.1
Ice	6.94	.93	0.4	0.1
Moving	2.06	1.28	0.1	0.1
Other	.70¶	.14	......	......
Furnishings	76.05	36.42	4.5	2.7
Care of the person	26.05	34.42	1.5	2.5
Barber	12.37	13.72	0.7	1.0
Cleaning supplies	13.68	20.70	0.8	1.5
Leisure time	61.82	89.54	3.6	6.6
Movies	5.55	14.82	0.3	1.1
Other commercial amusements	1.09	7.93	0.1	0.6
Newspapers	12.06	4.15	0.7	0.3
Other reading matter	1.66	1.13	0.1	0.1
Radios—payments	6.26	11.59	0.4	0.9
Upkeep and other musical instruments	6.24	4.28	0.4	0.3
Vacation	2.59	4.72	0.1	0.3
Tobacco	19.08	16.43	1.1	1.2
Gifts	5.66§	6.03	0.3	0.4
Stationery and postage	1.63	2.59	0.1	0.2
Other	......	15.87	......	1.2
Automobile	76.78	41.26	4.5	3.1
Other transportation	41.08	25.78	2.4	1.9
Carfare	37.40	20.19	2.2	1.5
Travel	3.32	5.41	0.2	0.4
Bicycles	.36	.18	......	......

* Excluding savings and investments.

† Including eight dependent relatives for whom clothing was purchased.

‡ The excess of owners' payments over rental value of the house (av. $137) has been classified as savings. Garage rent has been included here.

¶ Property insurance only.

§ Presents of money to relatives are classified with gifts.

TABLE 37—(*Continued*)

Item	Average annual expenditure per family		Percentage of total expenditure	
	Ford employees	San Diego Mexicans	Ford employees	San Diego Mexicans
Insurance—life and accident	$59.64	$32.14	3.5	2.4
Medical care	64.23	28.51	3.7	2.1
Doctor	38.17	15.49	2.2	1.1
Dentist	10.74	2.71	0.6	0.2
Drugs	8.99	4.81	0.5	0.4
Hospital	4.80	3.65	0.3	0.3
Other	1.53	1.85	0.1	0.1
Association dues	1.05‖	3.57	0.1	0.3
Education	9.02	8.34	0.5	0.6
School expenses	6.41	2.76	0.4	0.2
Lessons	2.61	5.58	0.1	0.4
Charity	11.15	14.31	0.7	1.1
Dependents	**	9.29	......	0.7
Church	9.62	3.76	0.6	0.3
Charitable agencies	1.53	1.26	0.1	0.1
Miscellaneous	5.96	38.84	0.3	2.9

‖ None of these men belonged to unions.
** Families with dependent relatives were excluded from the study.

Nesbitt standard allowance used in the present study by 15 per cent. Moreover, the Ford employees apparently spent their food allowance more wisely than did the Mexicans, with a greater emphasis on milk products, fruit, vegetables, and meat, and less emphasis on dry groceries.

The Detroit families were better housed as well as better fed. The average family occupied a separate house of four or five rooms, one room per person, whereas the Mexicans with an average of one more person per family lived in a three- or four-room house. The average annual rent in Detroit was nearly twice as great, $391 as against $213 in San Diego. Bathrooms were equally common in both studies. Thirty-two of the Ford employees were buying their houses, in contrast to thirteen of the Mexicans.

The man and wife in the average Detroit family spent slightly more for clothing than did the Mexicans, but their wardrobes, replacements, and prices were strikingly similar. The Ford employees were a trifle better dressed, since the man's suits and shirts, the woman's dresses and hats, were replaced a little more frequently, but the basic wardrobes were practically identical.

The average Mexican family with an income $375 a year less than the average Detroit family spent actually more on amusements ($90 Mexicans, $62 Detroit). It spent more than three times as much for movies and commercial amusements. In Detroit it was chiefly the children who patronized movies, but this was not true of the Mexicans. Nearly twice as many of the Mexicans were buying radios. Every Detroit family took a newspaper, but only half the Mexicans.

The Mexicans' bill for toilet supplies and cosmetics was larger. Fifty-nine Mexican families sent out laundry at some time in the year, in contrast to twenty-two of the Detroit families.

Forty-seven of the Ford employees owned an automobile, and only twenty-six of the Mexicans. A greater number of Detroit families carried life insurance and the premiums were larger. Thirty-seven of the, Detroit families managed to save an average of $134 during the year; twenty-five Mexican families saved an average of $109. Practically every Detroit family had some bill for medical care and the average bill was more than twice as large as that of the average Mexican family. The average Detroit purchase of furniture and furnishings was more than twice as large as that in San Diego.

One-third of the Mexican families were making some contribution to relatives outside the household. All families with dependents were excluded from the Detroit study.

With the exception of the allowance for dependents, the general scheme of expenditure of the Ford employees, so far as it differs from that of the Mexicans, is that of a more settled group, better fed, better housed, better prepared against catastrophe, probably paying all their doctors' bills, and spending less for amusements and the more frivolous items of expenditure.

Mexico, 1930—government employees.[64]—In 1930 the Oficina de Estudios Económicos of the Mexican National Railroads undertook to examine the living costs of employees of the Department of

---

[64] Ferrocarriles Nacionales de México, Oficina de Estudios Económicos, *Un estudio del costo de la vida en México*, Estudio número 2, Serie A.

the Treasury, who might be considered representative not only of all government office workers with similar salaries but of the whole Mexican middle class. For purposes of comparison with the San Diego study we shall consider only those groups of families[65] with three to five and six to eight members whose total income amounted to 1200–1800 pesos, or approximately \$480–\$720, the groups which most closely approach the San Diego Mexicans in size of family and of income, when the relative cost of living of the two countries is taken into consideration. Comparison has also been limited to results from the Distrito Federal, which included half the cases in the whole study. Where data were not classified by income and size of family, the results for all families studied in the district have been cited as being at least suggestive.

Comparison with this study does not, unfortunately, provide a contrast between the manner of living of the Mexican families in San Diego and the way they would live if they were at home, since it deals with the middle class instead of low-skilled wage earners. It indicates, however, the similarities and differences in expenditure between a standard of living in Mexico higher than working-class families could expect to reach and the standard which American wage scales enable them to maintain in this country.

The percentage distribution of expenditure[66] in the two groups shows two notable differences—a much smaller relative expenditure for food by the San Diego Mexicans, and the expenditure of an appreciable proportion of their income for items which would not occur in a working-class family budget in Mexico. The Mexican government employees devoted half or more of their total expenditure, depending on the size of family, to food; San Diego families about one-third. The proportion spent for clothing was about the same in both groups. The middle-class Mexicans at home spent 3

---

[65] By definition in this study, "family" included all members of the household except servants. No information was given on the composition of the average family or the number of wage earners. The average household in the Heller Committee study contained six persons.

[66] The classification used is that of the Oficina de Estudios Económicos. Greater detail was not available for that study. The absence of exact information on the relative costs of living in Mexico and in the United States made it seem inadvisable to attempt a comparison of actual monetary expenditures.

TABLE 38

PERCENTAGE DISTRIBUTION OF EXPENDITURES BY MEXICAN GOVERNMENT
EMPLOYEES, 1930, COMPARED WITH SAN DIEGO MEXICANS

Item	Percentage of total expenditure*		
	Mexican government employees		San Diego Mexicans
	Families of 3-5	Families of 6-8	
Total expenditure..............................	100.0¶	100.0¶	100.0†
Food..	50.1	57.0	37.6
Clothing....................................	12.2	11.3	14.0
Housing.....................................	14.2‡	11.1‡	16.4
House operation and furnishings......	7.9§	7.1§	8.5
Culture and diversions...................... (movies and theaters, excursions, education, reading matter, organization dues)	4.9	4.6	3.0
Extraordinary expenses...................... (medical, taxes, insurance premiums, repairs to owned house, travel, automobile)	2.9‡	3.0‡	8.3
Personal expenses............................. (tobacco, transportation—not journeys—barber, personal cleaning supplies, expenditures in *cantinas*)	7.8	5.9	5.2
Other.. (radios and other musical instruments, gifts, stationery and postage, miscellaneous leisure-time activities, charity, miscellaneous)	....	....	7.0

* Regardless of number reporting.

¶ The percentage distribution, given in terms of income in the original study has been re-computed on the basis of total expenditure to agree with the Heller Committee study.

† Excluding savings and investments.

Fire insurance, taxes, and repairs to house, which are classified under housing in Heller Committee studies, are here included under extraordinary expenses.

§ Costs of telephone, moving, and purchases of furniture other than bed linen, china, etc., were accidentally omitted from the schedule.

per cent for "extraordinary expenses," of which 2 per cent went to
the doctor, but the working-class Mexicans in San Diego spent over
8 per cent for this group of items, of which 3 per cent was for auto-

mobiles—26 per cent of the San Diego Mexicans owned cars, only 2.6 per cent of all the government employees in the Distrito Federal, including the highest incomes[67]—and 2.4 per cent for life insurance. Seven per cent of the average San Diego budget was spent on items which do not appear in the Mexico study, some accidentally omitted from the schedule, others, like radios, miscellaneous amusements, and support of dependents in the old country, characteristic of life in the United States. Although the San Diego Mexicans were of the working class and the government employees of Mexico represented the middle class, home-owning was more common among the former. Thirteen per cent of the San Diego Mexicans owned or were buying their homes, only 10 per cent of all income groups in the Distrito Federal; and this is probably a higher proportion than would be found in the Mexican middle class as a whole because of the facility for borrowing from the government pension fund.

The average government employee's family showed a considerable deficit between income and expenditure. According to the report, a large part of this was genuine and not due to errors of estimation. The deficit was probably explained by loans from more fortunate relatives and friends, unpaid rent, debts that run on forever, and graft money. The Mexicans in San Diego, with fewer credit resources, had fewer debts and deficits.

The government employees' budgets showed certain expenditures peculiar either to the social group or to Mexican life as contrasted with life in this country. Nearly 2 per cent of the average budget was spent for organization dues, because public employees were obliged to contribute a week's earnings each year to the Partido Nacional Revolucionario. Dues to all organizations cost the San Diego families 0.3 per cent a year. The other items included in the category "culture and diversions"—movies, education costs, reading matter, etc.—constituted about the same share of the family budget in both groups.

---

[67] The figure for the group with incomes of 1200–1800 pesos would undoubtedly have been even smaller.

In the smaller families in Mexico in which there was some surplus, expenditures for the category "personal expenses" were appreciably larger than among the San Diego Mexicans. This probably results from the item "expenditures in *cantinas*."

In general, the chief differences between the budgets of middle-class Mexicans at home and emigrant working-class Mexicans appear to be that the latter spent proportionately much less for food and more for distinctively American secondary expenses such as automobiles and radios.

VIII

CASE HISTORIES

The following six individual budgets are appended to illustrate by direct example the spending habits and family circumstances within this group of Mexican families. The examples selected include: (1) the details of a poverty standard for a day laborer with four young children, who was employed only forty weeks in the year; (2), (3), (4) three families with incomes of $2000 or more, differing greatly among themselves, one clinging to Mexican customs, one a modern, Americanized young couple, and the third a large family supported chiefly by the earnings of the older children; (5) a fisherman's family of eight, reported to live in typical Mexican fashion; and (6) a family selected as expressing the group average in size, income, and distribution of expenditure.

1. FAMILY NUMBER 6

The man, forty-seven years old, and the wife, thirty-eight, were both born in Mexico, as were the two eldest daughters, aged nine and seven; the two youngest, three years and eight months old respectively, were born in California. The man spoke and read English; the wife did not.

This family was living in poverty. Six persons were dependent on the man's earnings during forty weeks of the year as a day laborer, amounting to $748. They were overcrowded and undernourished and had little else than bare necessities.

Although one-half of the family budget went for food, the expenditure was far below minimum standard requirements. It was supplemented to some extent by discarded fish from the boats. Tortillas were served twice a day, frijoles always at lunch and often at dinner. The latter meal usually consisted of meat, fish or eggs, and one vegetable, usually potatoes. Nearly 30 per cent of the food allowance was spent for milk.

The flat, renting for $9 a month, contained three rooms for five people and a baby, no bathroom, an outside water-closet shared by three families.

FAMILY NUMBER 6

INCOME

Total income....$748.00	Man's earnings........$748.00	Reported deficit, $11.09 (error of estimation)

EXPENDITURE

Item	Amount		Percentage	
Total expenditure...	$ 759.09		100.0	
Food (meals at home)................................	380.64*		50.1	
Clothing..	111.95		14.8	
Man..		$34.35		4.5
Wife..		27.00		3.6
Children (4)...		50.60		6.7
Rent...	108.00†		14.2	
House operation...	59.50		7.8	
Electricity and gas...............................		33.70‡		4.4
Cleaning and laundry supplies..................		25.80		3.4
Care of the person (barber for man).............	4.20		0.6	
Furnishings...	30.00		4.0	
Sewing machine..		28.00		3.7
Minor items..		2.00		0.3
Leisure time...	21.80		2.9	
Amusements (not specified).......................		6.00		0.8
Tobacco...		7.80		1.0
Spending money for children.....................		8.00		1.1
Transportation (carfare)...............................	10.00		1.3	
Medical care (man).......................................	33.00¶		4.3	

* 37.3 per cent below standard.   ‡ Wood free.
† Includes water costs.   ¶ Other medical service free.

The family purchased, within the year of this study, a sewing machine, a profitable investment, since the mother made most of the family garments. She and the husband purchased almost complete outfits of clothing for $34 and $27 respectively. The children's shoes cost $1 a pair, and other articles were purchased on the same price scale.

Costs of house operation were limited to electricity, gas, and laundry soap and supplies. There was no household service, nor any laundry sent out, even though a child was born. The family bought no toothbrushes, no toothpaste, toilet soap, drugs, cosmetics, or shaving supplies, depending entirely on laundry soap for their personal cleansing.

The man spent $33 for a doctor when good advice would have sent him to a clinic. The mother must have received free care when the child was born, although none was reported. The older children were innoculated against diphtheria by the school nurse.

The family went to no movies, unless the tickets were purchased out of the children's spending money, and spent within the year only $6 for other amusements.

There was no provision for the future, neither insurance nor savings, but the family was not in debt.

2. FAMILY NUMBER 100

The family consisted of the father, thirty-one years old, the mother, aged twenty-eight, a boy of ten, girls of nine and seven, and the wife's semi-dependent parents, forty-six and forty-four years old, all born in Mexico.

This family represents the successful immigrants who have made money in the new country without making any very radical change in their standards of living. The man was a contracting brick-mason whose net profits were $2500 in 1929–30, the highest income of any family in the study. Nevertheless, the allotment for food was 37 per cent less than the minimum standard, and the house which they were purchasing had been converted into such as "might be found among the middle class any where in Spanish-speaking America," with a high-fenced yard in which were a vegetable garden, chickens, a goat, a kettle for boiling water, and a pile of firewood. "Everything was orderly and clean, with a decidedly exotic air." With a comfortable income they did not use their surplus to get better food or to lighten the woman's household duties by occasional domestic service or laundry sent out.

FAMILY NUMBER 100

INCOME

Total income..$2500.00	Man's earnings......$2500.00	Reported surplus $6.70
		Cash on hand...... 20.00
		Error of estima-
		tion.................. 13.30

EXPENDITURE

Item	Amount		Percentage	
Total expenditure...	$2493.30		100.0	
Food..	608.00		24.4	
Meals at home....................................		$520.00*		20.9
Meals bought (husband)............................		40.00		1.6
Grapes for wine............................		20.00		0.8
Sweets, etc., for fiestas............................		10.00		0.4
Feed for chickens and goat......................		18.00		0.7
Clothing..	302.00		12.1	
Man.....................................		99.75		4.0
Wife.....................................		83.40		3.3
Children (3)............................		118.85		4.8
Housing (purchasing)......................	729.00		29.3	
Installments and interest............................		640.00		25.7
Taxes and assessments..............................		65.00		2.6
Water.....................................		14.00		0.6
Repairs................		10.00		0.4
House operation...................................	35.50		1.4	
Electricity..		18.00†		0.7
Cleaning and laundry supplies..................		17.50		0.7
Care of the person....................	37.00		1.5	
Barber (man and children)........................		18.00		0.7
Personal cleaning supplies..................		19.00		0.8
Furnishings (minor items)............................	6.00		0.2	
Leisure time.......................	135.00		5.4	
Movies (4 persons)............................		24.00		1.0
Pool and billiards...........................		20.00		0.8
Newspaper........................		12.00		0.5
Tobacco.......................		26.00		1.0
Tuning piano............		10.00		0.4
Spending money for children......................		23.00		0.9
Gifts...............		15.00		0.6
Other (stationery, magazines)...................		5.00		0.2
Automobiles (2)—upkeep............................	353.00		14.1	
Transportation (carfare)............................	12.00		0.5	
Investments............................	159.80		6.4	
Insurance (5 persons)............................		59.80‡		2.4
Bank savings...........		100.00		4.0
Medical care (at clinic)............................	54.00		2.2	
Associations (union dues)............................	9.00		0.4	
Education (music lessons)............................	16.00		0.6	
Charity...........	37.00		1.5	
Dependents (sister-in-law in Mexico)........		25.00		1.0
Church...............		12.00		0.5

* 36.8 per cent below standard, but this deficiency is mitigated to some extent by garden produce, chickens and eggs, and goat milk, not included in cash expenditure.

  † Wood free.   ‡ $26 for man.

It is impossible on an income of $2500 completely to safeguard a family against the economic consequences of the wage-earner's death. These people with equity in a house, bank savings, and probably $1000 life insurance for the man were far better off than most of their compatriots.

They had adopted American working-class standards of dress; they owned two cars, one partly for business purposes; they patronized movies and poolrooms, gave the children spending money and music lessons, sent small sums to a relative in Mexico—lived, in short, according to their own ideas of comfort, if not luxury.

3. Family Number 93

The parents, twenty-eight and twenty-four years old, were born in Mexico, the two children, three and two years old, in California.

This family, also enjoying an income far above the average, was a direct contrast to Number 100 in its spending ways. "This is an up-to-date young couple .... in a furnished apartment; they seem to have all modern comforts." The man worked in an office as commission agent, at $150 a month, and the wife also did office work for part of the year, leaving the children at a day nursery. Both parents could read and write English. The family lived in a two-room furnished apartment, with a private bathroom, gas, hot-water heater, electricity—the very antithesis of the back-yard pile of driftwood, and the kettle of frijoles common to most families of the study.

Their food allowance gave a comfortable margin over the minimum standard, although it is impossible to tell how wisely they spent it. Their laundry was sent out regularly. The man, as an office worker, was required to dress better than a manual laborer, but his $185 clothing budget, including two $5 hats, a $35 overcoat and a $40 suit, $20 for shoe shines, and other items to scale, represented some degree of luxury above the minimum requirements of neatness. The woman's wardrobe, although of cheaper quality, was also above the minimum. She spent $8 for cosmetics.

Nearly 10 per cent of the family budget went into leisure-time activities—movies once a week, entertaining friends, purchasing a

FAMILY NUMBER 93

INCOME

Total income..$2016.00	Man's earnings......$1800.00 Wife's earnings...... 216.00	Reported deficit $25.15 (error of estimation)

EXPENDITURE

Item	Amount		Percentage	
Total expenditure............................	$2041.15		100.0	
Food..	600.50		29.4	
Meals at home.............................		$520.00*		25.4
Meals bought (husband's lunches).............		62.50		3.1
Beverages, etc..............................		18.00		0.9
Clothing..	388.15		19.0	
Man..		184.50		9.0
Wife..		132.50		6.5
Children (2).................................		71.15		3.5
Rent (furnished apartment)...............	307.50†		15.1	
House operation............................	91.30		4.5	
Gas and kerosene.........................		29.00		1.4
Telephone tolls............................		12.00		0.6
Cleaning and laundry supplies...............		12.80		0.6
Laundry (every 2 weeks).................		26.00		1.3
Moving..		11.50		0.6
Care of the person.......................	51.10		2.5	
Barber (whole family)...................		22.00		1.1
Personal cleaning supplies and cosmetics		29.10		1.4
Leisure time.................................	198.00		9.7	
Movies (parents)...........................		35.00		1.7
Pool and billiards.........................		15.00		0.7
Installments on radio....................		50.00		2.4
Tobacco.......................................		52.00		2.6
Social entertainment.....................		15.00		0.7
Magazines....................................		3.00		0.2
Photographs and toys....................		18.00		0.9
Stationery and stamps...................		10.00		0.5
Transportation.............................	35.00‡		1.7	
Carfare..		20.00		1.0
Travel..		15.00		0.7
Investments.................................	280.60		13.8	
Insurance (3 persons)...................		40.60		2.0
Bank savings...............................		120.00		5.9
Investments (real estate)..............		120.00		5.9
Medical care (dentist)..................	18.00		0.9	
Education (day nursery)................	25.00		1.2	
Charity..	26.00		1.2	
Dependents (mother in Mexico)................		25.00		1.2
Charity..		1.00		....
Incidentals..................................	20.00		1.0	

* Exceeds standard by 32.5 per cent.   ‡ Use of company car for Sunday excursions, etc.
† Includes electricity and water costs.

radio, $1 a week for tobacco, etc. The family had the use of the firm's automobile for excursions and picnics. The absence of automobile upkeep costs partly explains why these people could live in comfort, have their pleasures, and still invest 14 per cent of their income in insurance, bank savings, and real estate. An additional factor was the smallness of the family—two children instead of the average three or four.

4. Family Number 95

This family consisted of a father, aged forty-five, a mother, thirty-five, four girls of twenty, fifteen, thirteen, and ten, and two boys of nineteen and seventeen, all born in California.

This family had an income of over $2000, but it meant very much less in terms of well-being than in the case of two families already described, since the father's earnings constituted only one-third of the total income, the chief source being the earnings of the three eldest children, seventeen to twenty years old, and the mother. The income, therefore, had to care for the needs of a family of eight, three of whom were grown children with the responsibilities and demands of adults.

The father was a carpenter, employed only sixteen weeks in the year; the mother and eldest daughter worked half-time in the cannery for thirty-two weeks; the two boys were employed as mechanics' helpers for twenty-six and sixteen weeks, respectively. All the children turned their total earnings into the family purse and received back $1 a month for spending money.

The food allowance was 29 per cent below standard, not far from the average for the group. All meals were eaten at home or carried to work. The sample menus for two days included tortillas, frijoles, soup, and meat.

By the standards used in this study the family was adequately housed. For $23 a month it rented a six-room house with electricity, bathroom, and water-closet, and three bedrooms. No description of the condition of the house was given in the schedule.

The clothing bill was unusually large—one-fifth of the whole budget—because of the demands of five children in their 'teens.

FAMILY NUMBER 95

INCOME

Total income..$2036.40	Man's earnings......$768.00	Reported deficit..$96.00
	Wife's earnings...... 288.00	(error of estimation)
	Girl 20, earnings.... 288.00	
	Boy 19, earnings.... 390.00	
	Boy 17, earnings.... 158.40	
	Rental...................... 144.00	

EXPENDITURE

Item	Amount		Percentage	
Total expenditure..	$2132.40		100.0	
Food..	786.80		36.9	
Meals at home..		$774.80*		36.3
Feed for chickens.......................................		12.00		0.6
Clothing..	421.60		19.8	
Man..		38.00		1.8
Wife..		56.60		2.7
Working children (3).................................		181.50		8.5
Younger children (3).................................		145.50		6.8
Rent..	276.00†		12.9	
House operation...	108.40		5.1	
Electricity and kerosene...........................		54.00		2.6
Telephone—12 months..............................		39.00		1.8
Cleaning and laundry supplies.................		15.40		0.7
Care of the person...	35.80		1.7	
Barber (man and children).......................		14.40		0.7
Personal cleaning supplies and cosmetics		21.40		1.0
Furnishings..	118.00		5.5	
Installments (washing and sewing machines)...		95.00		4.5
Curtains and bed linen..............................		20.00		0.9
Minor items..		3.00		0.1
Leisure time..	78.80		3.7	
Movies (5 persons)....................................		20.00		0.9
Radio installments....................................		10.00		0.5
Newspaper...		10.80		0.5
Spending money for 3 oldest children........		36.00		1.7
Stationery and stamps..............................		2.00		0.1
Automobile—upkeep......................................	212.00		10.0	
Transportation (carfare)..............................	5.00		0.2	
Insurance (man—20-year endowment).........	21.00		1.0	
Medical care (at clinic)................................	30.00		1.4	
Dentist..		25.00		1.2
Drugs...		5.00		0.2
Education...	15.00		0.7	
School books..		5.00		0.2
Music lessons...		10.00		0.5
Charity (church)..	24.00		1.1	

* 29.1 per cent below standard; supplemented by a few home-grown vegetables, chickens, and eggs.
† Includes water costs.

The family's habits of spending inclined toward many very cheap articles. The eldest girl, for example, bought three hats at $1, two coats at $10, three dresses at $5, and three pairs of shoes at $3.50. Each of the three elder girls bought, within the year, 10 pairs of silk stockings at $1 or less.

The largest single item after food, clothing, and rent was the cost of running the family automobile, $212 a year, or 10 per cent of the total income. The next was furnishings, 5.5 per cent, which included $95 in installments on a washing machine and a sewing machine. Installments on a radio amounted to $10. The fuel bill was large, because all cooking was done on a kerosene stove. This was one of the seven families having a telephone.

The proportionate share of most of the other items was below average. This was notably true of leisure-time activities, for which the automobile was probably an alternative, provision for the future, which was limited to a small insurance policy for the man, and bills for dental care at a clinic.

5. FAMILY NUMBER 50

The father, twenty-eight years old, the mother, twenty-six, and the two elder girls, aged seven and six, were born in Mexico. The younger girls, four and three years old, and the baby boy of six months, were born in California. The household also included the wife's elder sister, who paid board and lodging and helped with household tasks.

The family was selected because it was described by the investigator as living in typical Mexican country style, so far as it can be transplanted to an alien environment.

The father was a fisherman, frequently absent on trips. His earnings, a percentage of the profits, were irregular, but probably averaged $20 a week throughout the year. When at home, he supplemented the food purchased by fish and other produce from the wharfs. The family never bought meat. Because of the man's absences it was impossible to determine the cost of a standard diet for this family. The expenditure for food was almost certainly below standard.

The family of eight lived in a four-room house at the rear of a vacant lot, renting for $15 a month. It had electricity, a water-closet on the porch, no bathroom, and no gas. Cooking was done with driftwood. The women ground their own meal for tortillas in a stone metate and baked the cakes on an iron plate over an open fire in the yard, exactly as if they were living in Mexico. The investigator reported: "their ideas of cleanliness and order are at least primitive."

The allowance for clothing was low, especially the $5 allowance for each of the younger children. But the children wore few clothes at home, the family received some gifts of clothing, and the mother was clever at making and remodeling.

The proportion spent for "necessaries" was below average; the unusually heavy items of expense were furnishings, medical care, savings, and amusements. The family had no automobile. During the year the family paid $30 in installments on a sewing machine, $35 for a bed and dresser, and $17 for other furnishings. The doctor and drug bills at the clinic were low, but the mother's two weeks in the hospital when the baby was born cost $75. In addition to $65 in premiums for small insurance policies for the parents and four older children, they saved $150, $80 of which was withdrawn to meet hospital expenses. Nine per cent of the budget, $121, was spent on leisure-time activities—movies about twice a month for the parents, $28 a year for other commercial amusements for the man, 50 cents a week for tobacco, 10 cents a week for chewing gum, 15 cents a week for the children's spending money. They bought a phonograph, and took a vacation visiting relatives on a farm below Tia Juana, which cost nothing but bus fare and spending money. In addition, $20 a year was reported for the husband's miscellaneous expenses.

The family afforded an excellent example of a standard of food, clothing, and housing which had not risen with income and therefore left a large surplus, half the total, for expenditure in other directions.

FAMILY NUMBER 50

Income

Total income..$1280.00	Man's earnings......$1040.00	Reported deficit $68.75
	Sister-in-law's	Drawn from sav-
	contributions.... 240.00	ings.................... 80.00
		Error of estima-
		tion...................... 11.25

Expenditure

Item	Amount		Percentage	
Total expenditure..	$1348.75		100.0	
Food...	376.65		27.9	
Meals at home...		$364.65*		27.0
Feed for chickens...		12.00		0.9
Clothing..	141.10†		10.5	
Man..		34.50		2.6
Wife...		44.40		3.3
Children (5)...		62.20		4.6
Rent...	180.00‡		13.3	
House operation...	30.80		2.3	
Electricity...		10.80§		0.8
Cleaning and laundry supplies.....................		14.00		1.1
Laundry while wife was in hospital............		6.00		0.4
Care of the person..	41.50		3.1	
Barber (whole family).................................		19.00		1.4
Personal cleaning supplies...........................		22.50		1.7
Furnishings...	82.00		6.1	
Installments on sewing machine.................		30.00		2.2
Bed and dresser...		35.00		2.6
Linoleum and blankets.................................		10.00		0.8
Minor items...		7.00		0.5
Leisure time..	120.70		8.9	
Vacation (family, 1 week)...........................		18.00¶		1.3
Movies (2 persons).......................................		15.00		1.1
Pool and billiards...		12.00		0.9
Sports events...		6.00		0.4
Games of chance...		10.00		0.8

* The father was so frequently absent on fishing trips that it was impossible to compute the number of equivalent adult males fed during the year. The cash expenditure was supplemented by eggs and rabbits, and by fish and other food from the boats.

† The sister-in-law paid for her clothing and all other expenses except board and room.

‡ Includes water costs.   § Wood free.

¶ Bus fare and spending money; visited relatives across the border.

FAMILY NUMBER 50—(*Continued*)

EXPENDITURE—(*Continued*)

Item	Amount		Percentage	
Leisure time—(*Continued*)				
Phonograph		$ 15.00		1.1
Tobacco		26.00		1.9
Chewing gum		5.20		0.4
Gifts		4.00		0.3
Spending money for children		7.50		0.6
Stationery and stamps		2.00		0.1
Transportation (carfare)	$ 12.00		0.9	
Investments	215.00		15.9	
Insurance (6 persons)		65.00		4.8
Savings		150.00		11.1
Medical care	97.00		7.2	
Doctor (clinic)		12.00		0.9
Drugs (clinic)		10.00		0.8
Hospital		75.00		5.5
Charity	32.00		2.4	
Dependents (father in Mexico)		20.00		1.5
Church		12.00		0.9
Incidentals (husband)	20.00		1.5	

6. FAMILY NUMBER 32

The father, twenty-eight years old, the mother, twenty-six, a girl of eight, and a boy of six were born in Mexico. The younger children, a boy of four and a girl of two, were born in California.

This family was chosen as the best example of the "average family." The parents were born in Mexico, and had been five years in this country. The wife could not read or write. The man read a little Spanish. There were four young children, and no other persons in the household. The father was employed as a laborer on a steady job with the gas company for forty-eight weeks of the year. His earnings constituted the entire family income, $1148, somewhat lower than the median for the group. The family had no automobile.

Expenditures for food and clothing were approximately average. The allowance for meals at home was 32.4 per cent below standard, but goat's milk, vegetables, and probably eggs from their hens, reduced, without entirely removing, the deficit. Home-made tortillas were served every day. The wife made many of the clothes for herself and the younger children. The man bought two hats in the year, two pairs of pants at $7, three overalls, six shirts at $2, two suits of underwear, twelve pairs of cheap socks, four pairs of shoes at $2.50, three ties at 50 cents, and spent $8 on shoe repairs and shines. The wife purchased three house dresses at $1, two better dresses at $3, four "corsets" at 50 cents, two suits of cheap underwear, six nightgowns, two pairs of silk stockings at 50 cents and four pairs of cotton at 25 cents, a pair of $4 shoes, and $2 worth of yard goods, probably for underwear, aprons, etc.

The family of six lived in a four-room house and slept in one room in two double beds. The large kitchen was used as a living room. Another room was set aside as the ceremonial "sala." The house was fitted with electricity, a bathroom, and a water-closet on the porch. Cooking was done with driftwood. The large back yard contained a shed for the goat, a patch of alfalfa, and a small vegetable garden. The house rented for $14 a month, not including water costs.

The costs of house operation were low, because no gas was used, although they included $20 for laundry sent out.

The father and the boy of six had their hair cut by the barber. The item of cleaning supplies was unusually low—two toothbrushes, six tubes of toothpaste, $4 for household drugs and antiseptics. Apparently the family washed and shaved with laundry soap and used no cosmetics.

The unusually high allowance for furnishings resulted from the purchase in ten installments during the year of a $65 living-room set for the "sala."

Eighteen per cent of the budget went for other items, chiefly movies, tobacco, and money sent to the man's mother in Mexico. The family went to the movies fifty times in the year. The man also spent $10 on pool and $39, twice the average allotment, for tobacco. The three elder children got 10 cents a week for spending money. Naturally, being illiterate, the adults bought no papers or magazines.

FAMILY NUMBER 32

INCOME

Total income, $1148.00	Man's earnings, $1148.00	Reported surplus $6.60
		Unpaid bills......... 10.00
		Error of estima-
		tion............... 16.60

EXPENDITURE

Item	Amount		Percentage	
Total expenditure..................................	$1141.40		100.0	
Food.........	465.00		40.7	
Meals at home..........		$416.00*		36.4
Meals bought (child's lunches)...............		16.00		1.4
Feed for goat and chickens......................		33.00		2.9
Clothing.............	151.60		13.3	
Man.........		60.50		5.3
Wife.........		22.70		2.0
Children (4)...............		68.40		6.0
Housing...........	180.00		15.8	
Rent.............		168.00		14.7
Water.............		12.00		1.1
House operation...............	49.90		4.4	
Electricity......		12.80†		1.1
Cleaning and laundry supplies...................		17.10		1.5
Laundry (20 weeks)...............		20.00		1.8
Care of the person.............	16.50		1.4	
Barber (man and one boy).....................		10.50		0.9
Personal cleaning supplies........................		6.00		0.5
Furnishings.............	76.00		6.6	
Living-room set............................		65.00		5.7
Blankets.............		9.50		0.8
Minor items.............		1.50		0.1
Leisure time.............	94.60		8.3	
Movies (3 persons).............................		30.00		2.6
Pool and billiards............................		10.00		0.9
Tobacco.........		39.00		3.4
Spending money for children......................		15.60		1.4
Transportation (carfare).............................	7.00		0.6	
Insurance (4 children)............................	20.80		1.8	
Medical care (at clinic)............................	18.00		1.6	
Doctor (clinic).............		6.00		0.5
Dentist (clinic).............		4.00		0.4
Drugs (clinic).............		8.00		0.7
Associations (union dues)............................	9.00		0.8	
Charity.............	41.00		3.6	
Dependents (mother in Mexico)................		30.00		2.6
Church.............		10.00		0.9
Charity.............		1.00		0.1
Incidentals (husband)...............	12.00		1.1	

* 32.4 per cent below standard, but supplemented by milk from the goat for 40 weeks, a few vegetables, and probably eggs and chickens, which reduce the deficit.

† Wood free.

The family had no automobile, and no carfare to or from work or school. Provision for the future was limited to very small insurance policies on the four children. In spite of four young children in the family the bills for medical care, received at a clinic, were only $18 for the year.

APPENDICES

APPENDIX A

CLOTHING DETAILS

A brief explanation of the derivation of the following tables seems desirable. The schedule called for an enumeration of the articles and cost of clothing bought for each member of the family during the year. It did not furnish any information about the stock of clothing already on hand, and without such information the wardrobe of different members of the average family could not be computed. Revisits to a number of families were planned in order to obtain inventories of the stock of clothing on hand. Clothing schedules were made up for persons of various age and sex groups—men, women, boys over twelve, girls over twelve, boys between two and twelve, girls between two and twelve, children under two. When an investigator was sent out in the fall of 1931, the shortage of funds made it necessary to limit the work to inventories for ten representatives of each of these seven groups. The investigator was instructed to select the individuals as far as possible from "typical" families of the earlier investigation. Upon the representative quality of this small sample depends the value of the column "stock" in the succeeding tables, and, to a less extent, the list of articles included.

As far as possible the tables include articles purchased by more than half the persons of the same age and sex group in the original study or appearing in more than half the wardrobes studied. The number of garments bought per year and the prices are based on the arithmetic average for all persons in the age and sex group; the unit price is based on the arithmetic average for persons reporting the article. The total annual cost in each case is close to the median for persons of that sex and age.

The results obtained from the two investigations were not wholly consistent. In the case of short-lived articles reported in the majority of wardrobes but purchased during the year by only a few persons of the original group, several explanations are possible. The group of ten reporting on their wardrobes may have had higher incomes and standards of dress. Articles such as handkerchiefs might have been gifts. Nightgowns and other garments might have been made from yard goods. Occasionally a new item had been added by a change in styles. Such articles were noted in the tables but no allowance made for replacement.

Another type of problem that arose was related to articles which might be substituted for each other, such as silk or cotton stockings. Frequently the balance of choices in the reports was so nearly equal that no true norm could be established, and the selection for inclusion in the "typical" wardrobe was necessarily arbitrary.

APPENDIX A 1

Stock and Annual Replacement of Clothing for a Man

Item	Stock on hand (base—10 persons)	Annual replacement	Unit price	Annual cost
		(base—100 families)		
Hat	1	½	$3.50	$1.75
Cap	1	⅓	1.75	.58
Lumberjacket*	....	....	....	....
Sweater	1	½	3.50	1.75
Suit	2†	¼†	26.00	6.50
Separate pants	2	1	3.50	3.50
Overalls	2	2	2.00	4.00
Shirts	4	4	1.15	4.60
Underwear	3	3	1.00	3.00
Nightclothes*	....	....	....	....
Socks	6	14	.25	3.50
Shoes	2	2½	4.50	11.25
Ties	2	1	1.00	1.00
Handkerchiefs	6	4	.15	.60
Garters*	....	....	....	....
Suspenders*	....	....	....	....
Belt	1	⅓	1.25	.42
Other items‡	....	....	....	....
Total replacements	....	....	....	42.45
Shoe repairs	....	1	1.50	1.50
Total cost				$43.95

* This item appeared in half or more of the wardrobes studied, but few or no purchases appeared in the original schedules.

† The stock is apparently inconsistent with the replacement figures.

‡ More than half of the 10 men reporting on their wardrobes owned at least one additional minor item.

APPENDIX A 2

STOCK AND ANNUAL REPLACEMENT OF CLOTHING FOR A WOMAN

Item	Stock on hand (base—10 persons)	Annual replacement	Unit price	Annual cost
		(base—100 families)		
Hat	2	1	$2.25	$2.25
Coat	1	½	18.00	9.00
Sweater	1	⅕	2.50	.50
Skirt or suit*	....	....	....	....
Blouses*	....	....	....	....
House dresses	3	3	1.00	3.00
Other dresses	2	1	9.00	9.00
Aprons	4	1⅓	.75	1.00
Corsets—girdle	2†	½	2.00	1.00
Underwear	3	3	.75	2.25
Nightclothes	3	¾	1.00	.75
Silk stockings	‡	3½	1.00	3.50
Other stockings	‡	3½	.50	1.75
Shoes	3	2	4.50	9.00
Scarf*	....	....	....	....
Handkerchiefs*	....	....	....	....
Handbag	1	¼	2.00	.50
Yard goods	....	....	....	1.50
Other items¶	....	....	....	....
Total cost	....	....	....	$45.00

* This item appeared in half or more of the wardrobes studied, but few purchases appeared in the original schedules.

† The stock is apparently inconsistent with the replacement figures.

‡ Because silk and cotton stockings are alternatives but have different wearing value, the evidence of 10 cases was too scattered to be conclusive. Each type was purchased by two-thirds of the 100 women.

¶ More than half of the 10 women reporting on their wardrobes owned at least one additional minor item.

APPENDIX A 3

STOCK AND ANNUAL REPLACEMENT OF CLOTHING FOR A BOY 12 OR OLDER

Item	Stock on hand (base—10 persons)	Annual replacement	Unit price	Annual cost
		(base—100 families)		
Hat*..................................	....	....	....	....
Cap..................................	1	1	$1.00	$1.00
Sweater..................................	1	1	2.75	2.75
Suit..................................	1	½	20.00	10.00
Separate pants..................................	2	1	2.75	2.75
Overalls..................................	2	2	1.25	2.50
Shirts..................................	4	4	.85	3.40
Underwear..................................	3	2½	.80	2.00
Socks..................................	6	11	.20	2.20
Shoes..................................	2	3	3.25	9.75
Handkerchiefs*..................................	....	....	....	....
Ties*..................................	....	....	....	....
Belt..................................	2	½	.80	.40
Suspenders*..................................	....	....	....	....
Total cost..................................	....	....	....	$36.75

* This item appeared in half or more of the wardrobes studied, but few purchases appeared in the original schedules.

APPENDIX A 4

STOCK AND ANNUAL REPLACEMENT OF CLOTHING FOR A GIRL
BETWEEN 2 AND 12 YEARS

Item	Stock on hand (base—10 persons)	Annual replacement	Unit price	Annual cost
		(base—100 families)		
Hat	1	⅓	$1.00	$ .33
Coat*	....	....	....	....
Sweater	2	¾	1.50	1.12
Skirt*	....	....	....	....
Middies*	....	....	....	....
School or house dresses	4	4	.75	3.00
Other dresses	1	½	2.00	1.00
Aprons*	....	....	....	....
Underwear	4	2½	.50	1.25
Nightclothes*	....	....	....	....
Socks	4	8	.25	2.00
Shoes	2	3½	2.50	8.75
Yard goods	....	....	....	1.50
Total cost	....	....	....	$18.95

* This item appeared in half or more of the wardrobes studied, but few purchases appeared in the original schedules.

APPENDIX B

AVERAGE EXPENDITURE PER FAMILY FOR SPECIFIED ITEMS REGARDLESS OF THE
NUMBER OF FAMILIES REPORTING SUCH EXPENDITURES

Items	Average expenditure per family	Percentage of total expenditure
All items	$1382.68	100.0
Food	506.58	36.6
Housing	221.06	16.0
Clothing	188.50	13.6
Leisure time	89.54	6.5
House operation	78.74	5.7
Investments	66.81	4.8
Automobile	41.26	3.0
Furnishings	36.42	2.6
Care of the person	34.42	2.5
Medical care	28.51	2.1
Transportation	25.78	1.9
Charity	14.31	1.0
Education	8.34	0.6
Associations	3.57	0.3
Other items	38.84	2.8

The Mexican American

An Arno Press Collection

Castañeda, Alfredo, et al, eds. **Mexican Americans and Educational Change.** 1974
Church Views of the Mexican American. 1974
Clinchy, Everett Ross, Jr. **Equality of Opportunity for Latin-Americans in Texas.** 1974
Crichton, Kyle S. **Law and Order Ltd.** 1928
Education and the Mexican American. 1974
Fincher, E. B. **Spanish-Americans as a Political Factor in New Mexico, 1912-1950.** 1974
Greenwood, Robert. **The California Outlaw:** Tiburcio Vasquez. 1960
Juan N. Cortina: Two Interpretations. 1974
Kibbe, Pauline R. **Latin Americans in Texas.** 1946
The Mexican American and the Law. 1974
Mexican American Bibliographies. 1974
Mexican Labor in the United States. 1974
The New Mexican Hispano. 1974
Otero, Miguel Antonio. **Otero: An Autobiographical Trilogy.** 1935/39/40
The Penitentes of New Mexico. 1974
Perales, Alonso S. **Are We Good Neighbors?** 1948
Perspectives on Mexican-American Life. 1974
Simmons, Ozzie G. **Anglo-Americans and Mexican Americans in South Texas.** 1974
Spanish and Mexican Land Grants. 1974
Tuck, Ruth D. **Not With the Fist.** 1946
Zeleny, Carolyn. **Relations Between the Spanish-Americans and Anglo-Americans in New Mexico.** 1974